Contents

Probably because the song lyrics were printed in the worship bulletin on this particular Sunday, I noticed a phrase I had somehow previously overlooked. The young soprano soloist, accompanied by smooth and steady runs from the piano and clear and graceful lilting from the flute, sang with confidence and joy. The sounds coming from three different sources blended beautifully and perfectly into one, no doubt calming the inner storms of many earnest worshipers.

The song "How Can I Keep From Singing" has always been a favorite. The tune is peaceful, restful, and hopeful, quietly but decisively overcoming the worst-case scenarios the lyrics describe. It does not matter what happens: tumult, strife, tempest, darkness, or storm. It does not matter our circumstances: "prison cells and dungeon vile"; we can nonetheless "hear the real, though far-off hymn that hails a new creation." Whatever harsh, hard, loud, and fearsome situations we may face, the lyrics proclaim, "No storm can shake my inmost calm while to that Rock I'm clinging."[1]

Then I heard the next phrase in that refrain: "Since love is Lord of heaven and earth, how can I keep from singing?" Love is Lord. Love—God—is in control. Love—God—will win.

If I had to choose a theme song for this quarter's lessons, this would be it. Our lessons, written by Sarah McGiverin, invite us to consider God's love in specific ways: its everlasting, caring, saving nature; its pervasive, preserving, renewing, and sustaining character. Its fullest expression we especially celebrate this season, when we boldly affirm, "God so loved the world that he gave his only Son, so that everyone who believes in him won't perish but will have eternal life" (John 3:16). Love, not death, is in control. Love—God—wins then, now, and in the future.

"Since love is Lord of heaven and earth, how can [we] keep from singing?"

How, indeed?

Jan Turrentine

Jan Turrentine
AdultBibleStudies@cokesbury.com

[1] *The Faith We Sing*, 2212.

MOUNTAINS OVERLOOKING THE SEA OF GALILEE

Adult Bible Studies

Spring 2017

God Loves Us

Uniform
Series
INTERNATIONAL BIBLE LESSONS
FOR CHRISTIAN TEACHING

Adult Bible Studies

Spring 2017 • Vol. 25, No. 3

Editorial and Design Team
Jan Turrentine, Editor
Tonya Williams, Production Editor
Ken M. Strickland, Designer

Administrative Team
Brian K. Milford, President/CEO
Marjorie M. Pon, Editor, Church
School Publications

ADULT BIBLE STUDIES (ISSN 0149-8347): An official resource for The United Methodist Church approved by The General Board of Discipleship and published quarterly by Cokesbury, The United Methodist Publishing House, 2222 Rosa L. Parks Blvd., P. O. Box 280988, Nashville, Tennessee 37228-0988. Copyright © 2016 by Cokesbury. Send address changes to ADULT BIBLE STUDIES, 2222 Rosa L. Parks Blvd., P. O. Box 280988, Nashville, Tennessee 37228-0988.
To order copies of this publication, call toll free: **800-672-1789**. FAX your order to **800-445-8189**. Telecommunications Device for the Deaf/Telex Telephone: **800-227-4091**. Automated order system is available after office hours, or order through Cokesbury.com. Use your Cokesbury account, American Express, Visa, Discover, or MasterCard.
For permission to reproduce any material in this publication, call 615-749-6268, or write to Permissions Office, 2222 Rosa L. Parks Blvd., P. O. Box 280988, Nashville, Tennessee 37228-0988. Scripture quotations in this publication, unless otherwise indicated, are from the Common English Bible, © Copyright 2011 by Common English Bible, and are used by permission. www.CommonEnglishBible.com. From the Revised English Bible, copyright © Cambridge University Press and Oxford University Press 1989. All rights reserved. New Revised Standard Version of the Bible, copyright 1989, Division of Christian Education of the National Council of the Churches of Christ in the United States of America. Used by permission. All rights reserved.
Lessons and Daily Bible Study are based on the International Sunday School Lessons for Christian Teaching, copyright © 2014 by the Committee on the Uniform Series.
ADULT BIBLE STUDIES is designed to help adults understand the meaning and authority of the Bible for Christian life. Daily study helps are published in *Daily Bible Study*. Leadership helps are published in *Adult Bible Studies Teacher*, and at AdultBibleStudies.com.
Cover Photo: Shutterstock

About the Cover

Mountains Overlooking the Sea of Galilee

The Psalms declare that all creation—sea, trees, rivers, mountains, every living creature—testifies to God's creating, renewing, sustaining, and saving love. David declared, "The LORD is my shepherd. I lack nothing. He lets me rest in grassy meadows; he leads me to restful waters" (Psalm 23:1-2). Jesus, the fullest expression of God's love, announced, "I am the good shepherd. The good shepherd lays down his life for the sheep" (John 10:11). This pastoral setting along the shore of the Sea of Galilee affirms Scripture's witness of the pervasive love God has for all creation.

MOUNTAINS OVERLOOKING THE SEA OF GALILEE

Adult Bible Studies

Spring 2017

God Loves Us

Uniform
Series

INTERNATIONAL BIBLE LESSONS
FOR CHRISTIAN TEACHING

Adult Bible Studies

Spring 2017 • Vol. 25, No. 3

Editorial and Design Team
Jan Turrentine, Editor
Tonya Williams, Production Editor
Ken M. Strickland, Designer

Administrative Team
Brian K. Milford, President/CEO
Marjorie M. Pon, Editor, Church
School Publications

ADULT BIBLE STUDIES (ISSN 0149-8347): An official resource for The United Methodist Church approved by The General Board of Discipleship and published quarterly by Cokesbury, The United Methodist Publishing House, 2222 Rosa L. Parks Blvd., P. O. Box 280988, Nashville, Tennessee 37228-0988. Copyright © 2016 by Cokesbury. Send address changes to ADULT BIBLE STUDIES, 2222 Rosa L. Parks Blvd., P. O. Box 280988, Nashville, Tennessee 37228-0988.
To order copies of this publication, call toll free: 800-672-1789. FAX your order to 800-445-8189. Telecommunications Device for the Deaf/Telex Telephone: 800-227-4091. Automated order system is available after office hours, or order through Cokesbury.com. Use your Cokesbury account, American Express, Visa, Discover, or MasterCard.
For permission to reproduce any material in this publication, call 615-749-6268, or write to Permissions Office, 2222 Rosa L. Parks Blvd., P. O. Box 280988, Nashville, Tennessee 37228-0988. Scripture quotations in this publication, unless otherwise indicated, are from the Common English Bible, © Copyright 2011 by Common English Bible, and are used by permission. www.CommonEnglishBible.com. From the Revised English Bible, copyright © Cambridge University Press and Oxford University Press 1989. All rights reserved. New Revised Standard Version of the Bible, copyright 1989, Division of Christian Education of the National Council of the Churches of Christ in the United States of America. Used by permission. All rights reserved.
Lessons and Daily Bible Study are based on the International Sunday School Lessons for Christian Teaching, copyright © 2014 by the Committee on the Uniform Series.
ADULT BIBLE STUDIES is designed to help adults understand the meaning and authority of the Bible for Christian life. Daily study helps are published in Daily Bible Study. Leadership helps are published in Adult Bible Studies Teacher, and at AdultBibleStudies.com.
Cover Photo: Shutterstock

About the Cover

Mountains Overlooking the Sea of Galilee

The Psalms declare that all creation—sea, trees, rivers, mountains, every living creature—testifies to God's creating, renewing, sustaining, and saving love. David declared, "The LORD is my shepherd. I lack nothing. He lets me rest in grassy meadows; he leads me to restful waters" (Psalm 23:1-2). Jesus, the fullest expression of God's love, announced, "I am the good shepherd. The good shepherd lays down his life for the sheep" (John 10:11). This pastoral setting along the shore of the Sea of Galilee affirms Scripture's witness of the pervasive love God has for all creation.

ADULT BIBLE STUDIES is available to **readers with visual challenges** through BookShare.org. To use BookShare.org, persons must have certified disabilities and must become members of the site. Churches can purchase memberships on behalf of their member(s) who need the service. There is a small one-time setup fee, plus a modest annual membership fee. At the website, files are converted to computerized audio for download to CD or iPod, as well as to other audio devices (such as DAISY format). Braille is also available, as are other options. Once individuals have a membership, they have access to thousands of titles in addition to ABS. Live-narrated audio for persons with certified disabilities is available from AUDIOBOOK MINISTRIES at http://www.audiobookministries.org/.

Sarah McGiverin is a freelance writer, with works published on Ministry Matters and by the General Board of Discipleship. She is a ministry consultant, helping pastors and other Christian professionals navigate vocational discernment and transition, with a special focus on worship leadership.

Sarah has served as a teaching assistant at Duke Divinity School and as a pastor on a rural two-point charge in Virginia. Before that, she was a tax preparer, a taxi cab driver, and a preschool teacher.

In her free time, Sarah enjoys knitting, hiking, spending time with her family, and volunteering at the local elementary school library. She lives and worships in Durham, North Carolina.

Daily Bible Study

February 27	Christ Died for Us	1 John 3:11-17
February 28	Jesus and the Father's Love	John 14:18-24
March 1	Believe in Jesus; Love One Another	1 John 3:18-24
March 2	The Spirit of God Confesses Jesus	1 John 4:1-6
March 3	Loving God and Brothers and Sisters	1 John 4:20–5:5
March 4	Thankful for God's Steadfast Love	Psalm 40:1-10
March 5	Dwelling in God's Love	1 John 4:7-19

The Source of All Love

Purpose

To confess that God is love and that this love is revealed in the lives of Jesus and of his followers

Hearing the Word

1 John 4:7-19

[7]Dear friends, let's love each other, because love is from God, and everyone who loves is born from God and knows God. [8]The person who doesn't love does not know God, because God is love. [9]This is how the love of God is revealed to us: God has sent his only Son into the world so that we can live through him. [10]This is love: it is not that we loved God but that he loved us and sent his Son as the sacrifice that deals with our sins.

[11]Dear friends, if God loved us this way, we also ought to love each other. [12]No one has ever seen God. If we love each other, God remains in us and his love is made perfect in us. [13]This is how we know we remain in him and he remains in us, because he has given us a measure of his Spirit. [14]We have seen and testify that the Father has sent the Son to be the savior of the world. [15]If any of us confess that Jesus is God's Son, God remains in us and we remain in God.

[16]We have known and have believed the love that God has for us. God is love, and those who remain in love remain in God and God remains in them. [17]This is how love has been perfected in us, so that we can have confidence on the Judgment Day, because we are exactly the same as God is in this world. [18]There is no fear in love, but perfect love drives out fear, because fear expects punishment. The person who is afraid has not been made perfect in love. [19]We love because God first loved us.

Key Verse: Dear friends, if God loved us this way, we ought to love each other. (1 John 4:11)

Seeing the Need

Anyone could have guessed that the debate at annual conference would be heated. Delegates felt strongly about their intended vote for or against the controversial resolution. Regardless of their position, all those who spoke from the floor asserted that their opinion was motivated by love for those who would be affected by the resolution; but people disagreed about who was most vulnerable and how best to love them.

Later that evening, some delegates gathered for dinner and began to discuss the day's events. "I wonder," said Fred, "how well we can love anyone else if we can't love our sisters and brothers here at conference?"

Phyllis was surprised. "Well, of course, we all love one another! We don't have to agree with one another in order to love one another!"

Carol was not so sure. "But doesn't it matter *how* we disagree? If we imply that someone who disagrees with us is not a good Christian . . ."

Elton became impatient. "But what if those persons aren't good Christians? Is it the loving thing to do to let them persist in misleading themselves and others?"

Every Christian knows that we are supposed to love one another, but how can we know what love is? How well do we witness to that love in our church communities?

Living the Faith

God Is Faithful

When I was a child, if I became angry enough with my brother or sister to say, "I hate you," my father would intone, "If any one says, 'I love God,' and hates his brother, he is a liar; for he who does not love his brother whom he has seen, cannot love God whom he has not seen" (1 John 4:20, Revised Standard Version). This was a terrifying thought! How could I ever hope to attain to the love of God with such infuriating siblings?

Fortunately for us, God is faithful even when we are unfaithful. We are reminded of this whenever we participate in Communion, when the celebrant says, "When we turned away and our love failed, your love remained steadfast." We are reassured after our prayer of confession: "Hear the good news: Christ died for us when we were yet sinners; that proves God's love for us." These words from the Eucharist reinforce what we read from 1 John: "This is love: it is not that we loved God but that he loved us" (verse 10).

John makes it clear that we are to model our love for others on God's love for us. This is different from understanding God's love for us in the context of our love for others. God's love for us is more constant, more reliable, more of every good and true thing than our love can be. The better we understand God's love, the less we worry about whether God loves us.

I have an electric tea kettle. When I want boiling water—whether for tea, for instant oatmeal, or for heating up jar lids when I am making jam —my electric kettle gets the job done quickly and reliably.

I have been known to say, "I love my kettle." What I really mean is, "My kettle is useful to me, and it performs well consistently. My kettle pleases me." Regardless of my "love" for my electric kettle, when it stops working, I will not love it anymore. I may even say, "I hate this kettle!" after it fails me for the second or third time. Then I will throw it away. My love for my kettle is conditional; I will only love it as long as it is useful to me.

God's love for us is not like my "love" for my tea kettle. It is not based on our behavior or on whether we are useful to God. However, too often, our human love for other people is more like my love for my tea kettle and less like God's love for us.

Often, I have heard people quote John's words: "Perfect love drives out fear," but rarely will they continue, as John does: "because fear expects punishment" (verse 18). John is talking about something specific here. He is not saying that people are not good Christians if they suffer from anxiety or if they are afraid of being hurt by other people. Religious faith helps ease some people's fears, while others continue to struggle.

Instead, John is talking about God's love, which is the perfect love that drives out our expectation that God will punish us for our failings.

If we are fearful that a friend will abandon us in a time of need, that might be based on earlier experiences of another friend having done that very thing. Our fear might be excessive, or it might be in fact reasonable, but God will never abandon us. If we are fearful of God, then we have still more to learn about what it means to say "God is love."

Have you feared losing God's love? Were you able to find reassurance? How?

God Is Generous

"If God loved us this way" (1 John 4:11). In what way? In a generous and self-sacrificing way. Specifically, God's love is revealed in Jesus—in his birth, life, death, and resurrection—the perfectly loving response to our imperfect failure to love and live rightly. Instead of deciding to give up on us, God sent Jesus "as the sacrifice that deals with our sins" (verse 10).

When we think of Jesus' sacrifice, we often think of his crucifixion. That was indeed a great sacrifice. Death by crucifixion was painful and public and took a long time. Jesus was cruelly executed, rejected by those he came to save, and abandoned by most of his friends.

However, Jesus' sacrifice began even earlier than that. In Philippians, Paul writes that becoming human was itself a sacrifice. In order for Jesus to be human, God the Son had to accept certain limits, or as Paul says, "He emptied himself" (Philippians 2:7; read verses 5-8). Being constrained by hunger and fatigue, or simply by being able to be in only one place at a time, for instance, must have been quite a sacrifice for a limitless God. God must love us very much to make so many sacrifices for us.

The Gospel of John includes a story about a woman who was caught in adultery. A group of men was prepared to stone her, in accordance with the Law. They asked Jesus his opinion of this. He told them, "Whoever hasn't sinned should throw the first stone" (John 8:7). One by one, the men all left, leaving only the woman with Jesus.

By the standard Jesus had given, only Jesus was qualified to throw the first stone because he was without sin, God the Son. Yet he said to the woman, "Neither do I condemn you" (John 8:11). He generously offered the woman forgiveness and a chance for a new start.

In Matthew 18:21, Peter asks Jesus, "How many times should I forgive my brother or sister who sins against me?" Jesus answered (as he so often did) with a story.

A king forgave a servant a debt so extravagant that it could never be repaid. That same servant found a fellow servant who owed him a much smaller (but still significant) sum. Instead of treating him with patience, the forgiven man had the other man thrown into debtor's prison. This made the king angry because the first servant had had so much mercy shown to him, but that servant somehow had failed to learn how to have mercy on others.

What have you learned from Jesus about God's love?

God Is With Us

"This is how we know," said John, and spoke about the Holy Spirit (1 John 4:13). When you are with a sister or a brother in Christ, if you are abiding in God's love, the Spirit is made manifest—obvious, apparent, observable. If we love as God loves, generously and unconditionally, then God is made visible in our life together.

John offers two parallel statements: If we love one another, then God lives in us; if we "confess that Jesus is God's Son," then God lives in us (verse 15). I wonder if, with these parallel verses, John was telling us that there is much more to a confession of faith than just words? If we do not love one another, are we denying that Jesus is God's Son? If I love Jesus, then am I not required to love all those for whom Jesus died? If I say, "God is love," what about my life demonstrates that belief to others?

This is just as difficult a prospect now as an adult as it was when I was a child. In the verse my father used to quote to me, the word *brother* means any brother or sister in Christ, not simply our biological siblings. Nevertheless, he used the Scripture appropriately: My own sister and brother were included in the broader category of those God would have me love.

Dad's word-play still serves as a reminder to me that I do not get to choose which people to love. God asks me to love those who are near at hand and far away, the ones most like me and the ones most unlike me, the most endearing and the most maddening to me, too.

Often, we might not embody God's love as well as we would like in our own lives and in our Christian communities. While we are aiming to be made perfect in love, most of us are not there yet. God is generous and faithful and continues to walk with us, encouraging us.

Sometimes, by God's grace, that love is made evident in miraculous gestures of love between people. It may be an almost private transformation, such as feeling our heart warm to a pew-mate we once found annoying. It may be more public, as when a person dedicates his or her life to a Christian mission of charity. Mother Teresa demonstrated this kind of love for the most impoverished people in Calcutta. Many others have turned their lives upside-down for love at home, by serving as a foster parent, for example.

While God's generosity is so great that there is no way we can match it, even small acts of generosity can serve as an homage to our generous God. Some days we may not act as generously, and others might wonder if we mean it when we say that God is love. This can be especially hurtful if we are doing the best that we can at the time. We may want to live in ways that demonstrate God's love, but for various reasons, we may find it difficult to do that in the same way that others might do. Everyone has different abilities, and even the same person will discover that his or her own abilities vary with time.

One way we can be generous and loving to our brothers and sisters in Christ is to give one another the benefit of the doubt. Only God can see into the heart of a person and know what they desire and of what they are capable. When a friend is not contributing to a ministry of the church or volunteering in a way that we think would best demonstrate God's love, or even when he or she seems to be wasting time or money doing things that are not wise, one generous response might be to first think, *This person is doing the best he or she can.* Another generous response would be to pray for the person.

This does not mean that we need to tolerate any kind of behavior. A nursery worker may well be doing the best she can; but if her best involves yelling at the children, then the loving thing to do is to relieve her of her responsibility for the nursery. God alone knows what love she has in her heart for the children, but we can do our best to act in a way to protect others from harm without casting judgment on the Christian character of another.

Because God is love and is the inspiration for our love, it is appropriate for us to consult God again and again as we learn to love those God has given to us to love. This quarter, we will be exploring the Scriptures to learn more about what God's love is and how God would have us respond in love.

As we study, I hope that we will all find ourselves inspired to spend time with God in prayer, asking for guidance in how to better love the people in our lives—people we encounter in person, as well as people we hear about through others. May God's love increasingly be revealed in all of our lives!

When is it particularly difficult to treat someone as a beloved child of God? When is it easy?

Loving God, you have loved us extravagantly. We especially see your love in Jesus—in his birth, life, and death. Yet sometimes it seems we have forgotten all about Jesus or do not think he is so important after all. Help us keep Jesus in the front of our minds so we can remember how loved we all are and so we can learn the best ways to love one another; in Jesus' name. Amen.

Daily Bible Study

March 6	God Be Merciful for Us Sinners	Luke 18:9-14
March 7	Justified by Faith	Romans 3:21-31
March 8	Christ Died for Sinners	Romans 5:6-11
March 9	Raised With Christ	1 Corinthians 15:12-25
March 10	Know the Love of Christ	Ephesians 3:14-21
March 11	Live Worthy of Your Calling	Ephesians 4:1-6
March 12	God's Overflowing Love	Ephesians 2:1-10

God's Overflowing Love

Purpose

To give thanks for the unearned gift of God's transforming love

Hearing the Word

Ephesians 2:1-10

[1]At one time you were like a dead person because of the things you did wrong and your offenses against God. [2]You used to live like people of this world. You followed the rule of a destructive spiritual power. This is the spirit of disobedience to God's will that is now at work in persons whose lives are characterized by disobedience. [3]At one time you were like those persons. All of you used to do whatever felt good and whatever you thought you wanted so that you were children headed for punishment just like everyone else.

[4-5]However, God is rich in mercy. He brought us to life with Christ while we were dead as a result of those things that we did wrong. He did this because of the great love that he has for us. You are saved by God's grace! [6]And God raised us up and seated us in the heavens with Christ Jesus. [7]God did this to show future generations the greatness of his grace by the goodness that God has shown us in Christ Jesus.

[8]You are saved by God's grace because of your faith. This salvation is God's gift. It's not something you possessed. [9]It's not something

you did that you can be proud of. ¹⁰Instead, we are God's accomplishment, created in Christ Jesus to do good things. God planned for these good things to be the way that we live our lives.

Key Verse: [God] brought us to life with Christ while we were dead as a result of those things that we did wrong. He did this because of the great love that he has for us. (Ephesians 2:5)

Seeing the Need

Evelyn saw her teenaged grandson bent over a notebook at the kitchen table. She was glad to see him so engrossed in his work. Fifteen minutes later, he was still scribbling away. "What are you working so hard on, B.J.?" she asked. "Something for school?"

B.J. looked up, startled, and shut his notebook suddenly. "It's nothing, Grandma. It's just my to-do list."

"There must be a lot on that list of yours. You were writing for a long time!" Evelyn sat down next to B.J. "I hadn't realized that you have so many things that you have to do. Are they all for school?" She reached over and took B.J.'s hand. "Is everything OK?"

"Sure, Grandma." B.J. looked away and sighed. "This is my to-do list for God. So I can become, I don't know, a better person. Good enough for God to like me, I guess. It seems impossible."

B.J. looked miserable. Evelyn had felt that way herself when she was younger; but now, when she grieved over her sins, she knew she could share that grief with God. "B.J.," she assured him, "there is nothing you can do that will make God stop loving you. God will always love you, and so will I!"

She wondered, though, if there was something more she should do or say for B.J. She resolved to pray about it.

Living the Faith

God's Love Is a Gift

The opening of Ephesians 2 may be uncomfortable for some of us to read. How do we understand the accusation that we were "like a dead person" before we were brought to life in Christ if we have been Christians for many years? Some of us might have difficulty identifying a time in which our lives were "characterized by disobedience" (verse 2).

Of course, when Paul originally wrote these words, he was addressing a particular community of first-century Christian converts. He had a particular "you" in mind—people who all had come to Christ as adults. So do these words even apply to those who have spent their whole lives in the church?

Think back over your life. How have you changed and grown? Are there things you did in the past that you would not do now? Are there decisions you made that seemed good when you made them, maybe even seemed righteous, but that you now see as being motivated by self-centeredness or self-preservation instead of by love and obedience to God's will?

Paul makes it clear in verse 3 that his words apply to everyone: The Ephesians behaved in this way "just like everyone else." We all have had times when we were disobedient to God's will.

Jesus' many problems with the Pharisees seem to have been rooted in their belief that they were doing everything right while everyone else was getting it wrong. In Matthew 9:11-13, we read about the Pharisees' complaint that Jesus ate with sinners. Jesus replied, "Healthy people don't need a doctor, but sick people do. . . . I didn't come to call righteous people, but sinners" (Matthew 9:12-13).

Was Jesus saying that he did not care about saving the Pharisees? Not at all! Instead, he was pointing out that the problem with the Pharisees was that they thought (erroneously) that they were healthy. They thought they did not need God's help because they were doing everything perfectly on their own.

This might be why, in the space between the two statements quoted above, Jesus said, "Go and learn what this means: *I want mercy and not sacrifice*" (Matthew 9:13; Jesus was quoting from Hosea 6:6.) Perhaps meditating on the prophets would lead some of the Pharisees to reflect on ways in which they had failed to act with mercy, and so they would discover that they, too, needed a doctor.

One way in which the Pharisees were unmerciful was in their assertion of their own unfailing righteousness. They failed to see how their rigorous standards left people out of God's plan. If behaving with absolute correctness was necessary for salvation, then those who saw themselves more clearly than the Pharisees might be led to despair. Those who knew that they were not unfailingly righteous were struggling and failing to earn God's love.

If the Pharisees had it all figured out, then only Pharisees could be saved, because most people find it impossible to be unfailingly righteous all the time. Jesus pointed out that this unfailing righteousness was impossible for the Pharisees, too. They just had not admitted it yet.

It takes a great deal of discipline to accept and give thanks for God's salvation as a gift that we do nothing to earn. It is difficult to understand this or even to want this to be true. Instead, it is more comfortable for us if we can figure out what we did for God to love us, or (if we do not already understand that God loves us) we are simply told exactly what we can do to get on God's good side.

Paul emphasizes that we do not make salvation happen. God does. God "brought us to life with Christ" (Ephesians 2:4) even when we were denying Christ. We might not think that we have ever denied Jesus; but even if we have never stopped proclaiming our love for Jesus with our words, there have been times in all of our lives when our actions did not match our words, when we were unmerciful, or when we were motivated by something other than love of God and neighbor.

All sorts of things can get in the way of our understanding of grace, God's free gift of saving love. One way is to fail to see that we need saving at all. Another is to think that there are steps we are obligated to take in order to save ourselves.

Do some people need God's love more than others?

Faith Is a Gift

Some of us know exactly when we came to faith, when we came to believe in God's saving love for us. Whether we grew up in the church or we joined as a teenager or an adult, many people can point to an event —a time in prayer; in Christian conversation; in a worship service; or around a campfire—when, like John Wesley, our "heart was strangely warmed" and we knew and accepted that Jesus died for us and that nothing would ever be the same for us again.

For others of us, coming to faith has been a process, deepening in understanding of certain aspects of the Scriptures and of Jesus' life and God's love. We have believed for a long time, and we cannot point to exactly when or how it happened. Then there are those of us for whom faith is a combination of these two: slowly growing and changing and learning, stimulated by an initial, spectacular, life-changing event or punctuated by more than one faith-kindling moment.

The Purpose Statement for this lesson states that God's love is an "unearned gift." This statement is inspired by today's Scripture, in which we read, "This salvation is God's gift. It's not something you possessed" (Ephesians 2:8), but that same verse begins, "You are saved by God's grace because of your faith." How do we fit these two ideas together? If we are saved because of our faith, then isn't that something we did to earn or deserve God's transforming love? Isn't faith a decision that we made; and if we are saved by our faith, aren't we being rewarded for that decision?

Think about your own story of how you came to faith in Jesus. Does it feel like a process or an event that you were in control of? Was it something that you did yourself? To what extent did you make a "decision for Christ"? How was God involved? What role do you believe the Holy Spirit played in your story?

Have you heard the term *prevenient grace*? *Prevenient grace* is the idea that God is working in our lives before we are aware of it. Every move we make toward God is in response to something that God has already done in us. Whatever part we play in coming to faith (and growing in faith), God creates the necessary conditions for our faith. Perhaps this is how Paul can follow his words about faith and salvation with verse 9: "It's not something you did that you can be proud of."

Is faith something that we do, something that God does, or something we do together with God?

Our Living Witness Is a Gift

In Lesson 1, we began talking about God's love as the inspiration for our own love. When we accept God's love for us, we find ourselves wanting to do things for God as a tribute to the one who loves us so much.

This is different from B.J. in the story above, who believed that he had to do certain things in order for God to love him. B.J. was acting out of fear that God's love was something nearly impossible to earn. Instead, when we understand that God's love precedes us in everything we do, living by God's commands becomes an act of gratitude.

Just as when we love a person (a parent, a child, a sibling, a spouse), we are not content with what we are already doing for God. However, we seek to learn more and live in a more pleasing way than we are doing today, not because we are worried about losing God but because we love God so much that we cannot help but desire to do more.

In Ephesians 2:10, Paul calls the readers "God's accomplishment" (another translation of the Greek might be "God's creation") and then expands on that idea, writing, "created in Christ Jesus to do good things." Not only is our faith a gift, but the good things we do are a gift. We were created in such a way that we are complete when we are behaving in certain ways. God's creation is brought to completion in us when we act in the way that God created us to act.

Like our salvation, this is not something for us to be proud of but something for us to be grateful for. Our faith has opened the door for us to live the life God desires for us: a life of love-inspired obedience to God's commands.

As the prayer of confession in the Communion ritual indicates, confessing that we need God and cannot live righteously without God's help "[frees] us for joyful obedience."[1] It is because we are encouraged by God's unconditional love and daily forgiveness that we are able to continue growing in love, putting that love into action.

What is something you are doing for God now that you have started doing recently (in the past couple of years)? What inspired you to make that change?

Christian Community Is a Gift

It is not only God's love that empowers us to act rightly in the world. Many things contribute to our ability to love and help others. Our health, our financial resources, the area in which we live, the training that we have—all of these things and more create opportunities for particular ways in which we can live as God's children in the world.

One thing we all need in order to live faithful lives is a community of support. God's love for us in Christ has created a community of people who have all recognized the importance of following Jesus. This is a great gift. In Christian community, we find the love, support, prayers, encouragement, inspiration, and accountability we need in order to live as new people.

Throughout this passage, Paul is speaking in the plural. Every time he uses the word "you," he is talking to a collective "you." This is difficult to translate into English without resorting to regional dialects. For instance, imagine this: "At one time, all y'all were like a dead person." Collectively, you were dead, as a body. Members of a dead body. Now, collectively, you are alive, as one body, the body of Christ.

Paul was not talking about individual faith and individual lives here. What might it mean to think about salvation in plural terms, to think of salvation in terms of our Christian communities?

Christian communities are one way in which God reaches out to humanity. Bible translations and Bible lessons are produced and published by Christian communities. Seminaries that train Christian leaders are themselves Christian communities. Christian communities provide Bible studies and Sunday school classes, fund church camps and mission trips, and provide many other environments and tools through which individuals come to faith. When you remember how you came to faith in Jesus, what role does a Christian community play in that story?

You are probably studying this lesson together with a group of other Christians, whether as part of a Sunday school class or a Bible study or some other small group. Paul's plural "you" reminds us that we are not created to be Christians on our own but that Christianity is a group activity. God knows that we need the love, encouragement, and prayers of others, and others need our love, encouragement, and prayers, too. What a marvelous gift God has given us in one another!

Think about the prepositions in, with, through, *and* by. *Which one (if any) do you think best fills in the blank in the following statement? "I am saved _____ my Christian community."*

Generous God, you have given us so many gifts—our lives, our talents, and our personalities. You have given us one another and salvation in Christ Jesus. Thank you for these many gifts. Help us to recognize your love for us in each of these gifts. Free us from our worry that we do not deserve your love and from our pride that we might somehow have earned it. Open our hearts to trust in your grace, your free gift of saving and transforming love; in Jesus' name. Amen.

[1]*The United Methodist Hymnal*; page 8.

Daily Bible Study

God's Love Manifested

Purpose

To identify the qualities of relationships rooted in God's love

Hearing the Word

John 15:1-17

[1] "I am the true vine, and my Father is the vineyard keeper. [2] He removes any of my branches that don't produce fruit, and he trims any branch that produces fruit so that it will produce even more fruit. [3] You are already trimmed because of the word I have spoken to you. [4] Remain in me, and I will remain in you. A branch can't produce fruit by itself, but must remain in the vine. Likewise, you can't produce fruit unless you remain in me. [5] I am the vine; you are the branches. If you remain in me and I in you, then you will produce much fruit. Without me, you can't do anything. [6] If you don't remain in me, you will be like a branch that is thrown out and dries up. Those branches are gathered up, thrown into a fire, and burned. [7] If you remain in me and my words remain in you, ask for whatever you want and it will be done for you. [8] My Father is glorified when you produce much fruit and in this way prove that you are my disciples.

[9] "As the Father loved me, I too have loved you. Remain in my love. [10] If you keep my commandments, you will remain in my love, just as I kept my Father's commandments and remain in his love. [11] I have said these things to you so that my joy will be in you and your joy will be complete. [12] This is my commandment: love each other just

as I have loved you. [13]No one has greater love than to give up one's life for one's friends. [14]You are my friends if you do what I command you. [15]I don't call you servants any longer, because servants don't know what their master is doing. Instead, I call you friends, because everything I heard from my Father I have made known to you. [16]You didn't choose me, but I chose you and appointed you so that you could go and produce fruit and so that your fruit could last. As a result, whatever you ask the Father in my name, he will give you. [17]I give you these commandments so that you can love each other.

Key Verse: This is my commandment: love each other just as I have loved you. (John 15:12)

Seeing the Need

If you have joined a United Methodist congregation, you were likely asked to "uphold it by your prayers, your presence, your gifts, your service, and your witness." What does this mean? *Presence* is pretty self-explanatory: You promised to show up for church functions.

How do we pray for a congregation? Do we pray for the individuals in the congregation? for its ministries? Are our gifts just the money we put in the offering plate, or does that mean our time and work on behalf of the church? If so, how is that different from our service? Does this mean service to the church or service to the community alongside other people from our church? Isn't all of this a witness? Is witness something extra we do in addition to prayers, presence, gifts, and service, or is it a way of understanding our gifts and service in a different way?

When we understand our lives in the context of Jesus' life, and when we try to align our desires with his desires, we might gain a new perspective on how to understand our membership vows. Is it possible that pledging our prayers, our presence, our gifts, our service, and our witness is just another way of pledging to serve one another in Christian love?

Living the Faith

Last Words

If you knew that you would die tomorrow and you had one last opportunity to talk with your friends and family, what would you want to say? What would be the most important things you would want them to know?

Today's Scripture includes some of Jesus' last words to his disciples, as recorded in the Gospel of John. "The Farewell Discourse" is the name Bible scholars have given John 13–17, the words Jesus spoke to his disciples on the evening before he was crucified. Of course, we know that Jesus' death was not final. He was resurrected on the third day; but after a short time with his disciples, he ascended to be with the Father in heaven. He would no longer be present with them in the same bodily way he had been during his earthly ministry.

Because these are "last words," it is tempting to compare them to other last words that people have spoken to us. I remember the last real conversation I had with my father, the weekend that hospice was called, and we all had to face that he was dying. There were things I wanted to ask him and things he wanted to tell me. You, too, may have memories of a significant last conversation with a parent, a grandparent, a spouse, or some other beloved person in your life.

Last words are rooted in an honest assessment of how little time is left together. These words can only properly be spoken when the time for denial is passed and it is clear that death is near. Last words often convey expressions of love. In these conversations, we express our emotions to one another more openly than perhaps we have done before. Last words may also carry instructions: a last opportunity for the dying person to convey things he or she hopes you will not forget, even if you do not have that person present to remind you of certain important principles and practices anymore.

These last words of Jesus are similar to other last words in these respects. Jesus warned the disciples that he would soon no longer be with them. He called the disciples his friends and emphasized his love for them. Jesus gave them instructions for how to live and how to love one another.

However, Jesus' words are different from our other experiences of last words, too. They are different in part because the disciples did not understand that they were last words. The disciples did not know that Jesus was going to die the next day. For them, these words would become last words only in retrospect. They are different in part because Jesus would get another opportunity to speak to the disciples after all, after the Resurrection.

Mostly, these words are different because they were spoken by Jesus, the Incarnate Son of God the Father. Jesus is God with us, and he continued to be God with us even after he was no longer physically present with the disciples. When Jesus instructed the disciples, "Remain in me" (John 15:4), with the parallel assurance that he would remain in them, he did not mean that they were to simply carry a warm and fuzzy memory of him to ponder periodically. What Jesus described—what Jesus can and does deliver—is a continuing direct connection.

Even though Jesus is no longer bodily present in the same way that he was 2,000 years ago in Galilee and Judea, he is present to us in an intimate and life-giving way. Our relationship with Jesus is different from our connection to any other person, whether they have died or are still living.

In what ways do you "stay connected" with Jesus?

One Will

No matter how kind, wise, or virtuous another human being is or was, it is neither safe nor wise to invest our entire being in that person. No person other than Jesus is strong and steady enough to be the vine that gives life to our lives.

"Without me, you can't do anything," Jesus said (John 15:5). In anyone else's mouth, these words would sound threatening and derogatory; but when Jesus speaks them, it is simply a statement of fact. We need Jesus in order to live fruitful lives. We connect to God through Jesus, and so it is through Jesus that we receive life and love and the strength to live the loving lives God intends for us.

Jesus compares the relationship that the disciples ought to have with him with his own relationship with God the Father. This is an incredible analogy. Jesus and God the Father are two persons of the Trinity—united (among other ways) in a common life, a common will, and a common purpose. Jesus also said that his love for the disciples was like the love the Father has for him. Jesus, in his life, death, and resurrection—and here in his words—invites humanity to participate in the love that constitutes the Triune God. The Trinity is not an entirely closed system; we are invited to share in the life of God.

Can we rise to the occasion? It is in Jesus' nature to keep the Father's commands. His will is substantially one with the Father's will. As for us mere humans, our will is often divided. Sometimes we desire to do what God wants us to do. Other times, we may not be thinking much about God when we make decisions. To remain in Jesus as Jesus remains in the Father may mean developing an all-the-time awareness of Jesus' will.

In the late 1990's, it became popular among some Christians to wear bracelets with the letters "WWJD" ("What Would Jesus Do?") on them. When taken literally, this may not be particularly helpful. There are a lot of things Jesus might do that we are unable to do. (For instance, coming across a homeless person on the side of the road, Jesus would most likely instantly cure her of whatever malady she suffered from. Usually, we do not have much more to offer than a sandwich, a bottle of water, and a prayer.) However, these bracelets were on the right track. Wearing a WWJD bracelet served for many people as a constant reminder to think about Jesus in every decision.

For others, wearing a cross serves a similar purpose. When we wear one, we know that others will know we are Christian, and so, hopefully, we remember to act accordingly.

Another way to align our will with Jesus is to pray. In addition to our prayers of thanks and our intercessory prayers (prayers on behalf of others), we can pray for ourselves that we will live lives rooted in Jesus. We can pray that throughout the day we will make decisions pleasing to God.

We can study the Scriptures so that we have a clearer idea of what God wants for us. At church, our will is shaped by the prayers we pray together, by the minister's sermons, by the hymns we sing, and by the discipline of stewardship. The relationships we form in Sunday school and in other small groups create accountability. We have Christian friends who can help us discern when we are doing God's will and when we are not.

When do you notice your desires diverging from God's desires? How do you get "back on track"?

Pruning Shears

Life does not become easy just because we are following Jesus' commandments. Jesus used the analogy of a grapevine: the branches that do not bear fruit are cut off, but the branches that do bear fruit are not left alone. They are cut back, sometimes severely, so that they will bear more fruit next season.

Our capacity for love increases when we remain in Jesus. We glorify God when we serve others, and when we work together with God to demonstrate that God is love. However, we are not spared all pain. Sometimes, old growth needs to be trimmed back, and that is not painless.

Being pruned is part of our life in Jesus. We may have experienced this pruning in many ways. One way may be the disappointment of a prayer not being answered in the way we expected.

Jesus said, "If you remain in me and my words remain in you, ask for whatever you want and it will be done for you" (John 15:7). Many of us have remarkable stories of miraculously answered prayers when we asked God for some specific blessing on a person or a group of people, and God not only did what we asked but did even more, going beyond anything we could have imagined happening.

However, most of us also have the experience of asking for some specific blessing that God did not then choose to bestow. It is not that we were not asking for something good (healing, a baby, a job, a mended relationship). How can we reconcile this with Jesus' words? We asked for what we wanted, and it was *not* done for us.

When we have not received something good for which we prayed, we can ask God to trim away our disappointment. Perhaps this is an opportunity to recognize something good that God was doing by not giving us what we asked for. Or perhaps that answer is impossible for us to see, and instead we learn through this experience that we still trust God no matter what happens. Or perhaps the best we can do is to acknowledge that God's ways are not our ways and God's thoughts are not our thoughts (Isaiah 55:6-13). However we deal with our disappointment, we require God's help to trim it back so that we can produce new growth and bear still more fruit.

When have you been delighted with God's answer to prayer? Have you always received what you asked God for?

Divine Love

God's will and God's love are inseparable. In John 15:10, Jesus tells his disciples, "If you keep my commandments, you will remain in my love, just as I kept my Father's commandments and remain in his love." When Jesus used the words "command" and "commandment" (which he did a lot in the Farewell Discourse), in general, he was talking about acting in accordance with the will/the desire of God. However, it seems that Jesus had specific commandments in mind, commandments about how to love one another.

In verse 12, he reminds the disciples, "This is my commandment: love each other just as I have loved you." I call this a "reminder" because Jesus had already spoken similar words in the Farewell Discourse, beginning with 13:34. This command was so important that Jesus repeated it again here in Chapter 15.

Loving one another as Jesus loved us is a tall order! The very evening that Jesus spoke these words, he was arrested. In less than 24 hours, he would go unresisting to a death that was a sacrifice of love not just for his disciples, nor even just for the people of Israel, but for all people—even people who had not yet been born, even for you and for me!

"No one has greater love than to give up one's life for one's friends," Jesus said that evening (verse 13). What could it mean to love one another as Jesus loved the disciples? It might well mean valuing our own lives no more than the lives of people who do not even understand us well and even infuriate us sometimes.

Jesus gave the disciples a concrete example of that kind of love earlier the same evening when he washed their feet. When he had finished washing their feet, he told them, "If I, your Lord and teacher, have washed your feet, you too must wash each other's feet" (13:14). If God-with-us could stoop to serve ordinary human beings, then who are we to reject any kind of service to others as "beneath us"?

Are there any kinds of work (around the house, at church, or elsewhere) that seem like a waste of your time or talents? Are there any kinds of work that you feel like you should not have to do, whether because of your age, your gender, your education, or your experience? If something needs to be done, you see that it needs doing, and you have the ability to do it, what stands in your way?

Similarly, in the Letter of James, we find these words: "My brothers and sisters, when you show favoritism you deny the faithfulness of our Lord Jesus Christ, who has been resurrected in glory" (2:1). Jesus showed his disciples that when we love one another, we serve one another, without reference to or regard for the relative "status" others would assign us. When we recognize that all people are equal recipients of God's loving care, then we see that no one person (or group of people) is more worthy of our attention than any other.

How has your "rootedness" in Jesus inspired you to serve others? What have you learned about love when serving others?

Father God, Jesus' desires are one with your own. Shape our hearts to be like your heart so that we will desire what you desire and love as you love, as Jesus taught us to do; in Jesus' name. Amen.

Daily Bible Study

March 20	The Prophesied Day of the Lord	Joel 2:1-11
March 21	The People Called to Repent	Joel 2:15-17
March 22	God Restores Land and People	Joel 2:20-27
March 23	Day of the Lord at Pentecost	Acts 2:14-21
March 24	The Final Day of the Lord	2 Peter 3:1-10
March 25	God Judges Nations; Proclaims Judah's Future	Joel 3:1-3, 18-21
March 26	Our Gracious and Merciful God	Joel 2:12-13, 18-19, 28-32

God's Love Restores

Purpose

To recognize that God sometimes opens windows of opportunity for us to repent and to repair relationships

Hearing the Word

The Scripture for this lesson is printed below. The background text is Joel 2.

Joel 2:12-13, 18-19, 28-32

[12]Yet even now, says the LORD,
return to me with all your hearts,
with fasting, with weeping, and with sorrow;
[13]tear your hearts
and not your clothing.
Return to the LORD your God,
for he is merciful and compassionate,
very patient, full of faithful love,
and ready to forgive. . . .
[18]Then the LORD became passionate about this land, and had pity on his people.
[19]The LORD responded to the people:
See, I am sending you
the corn, new wine, and fresh oil,
and you will be fully satisfied by it;and I will no longer make you
a disgrace among the nations. . . .

²⁸After that I will pour out my spirit upon everyone;
your sons and your daughters will prophesy,
your old men will dream dreams,
and your young men will see visions.
²⁹In those days, I will also pour out my
spirit on the male and female slaves.

³⁰I will give signs in the heavens and on the earth—blood and fire
and columns of smoke. ³¹ The sun will be turned to darkness, and
the moon to blood before the great and dreadful day of the Lord
comes. ³²But everyone who calls on the Lord's name will be saved;
for on Mount Zion and in Jerusalem there will be security, as the
Lord has promised; and in Jerusalem, the Lord will summon those
who survive.

Key Verse: Tear your hearts and not your clothing. / Return to the Lord
your God, / for he is merciful and compassionate, / very patient,
full of faithful love, / and ready to forgive. (Joel 2:13)

Seeing the Need

When four-year-old Billy became angry with his father for not taking him to the zoo, he promised he would never speak to his father again. Five minutes later, he was in the kitchen asking his father for a cookie.

When Doris became angry with her husband, George, for insulting her mother, there were no dramatic announcements; she simply stopped speaking to him. However, the next day, when he was rummaging through the garage, she could not help but call out, "You left the screwdriver on the kitchen counter."

Brandon's sister, Julie, lived in another state, so it was easy simply to stop calling her when she "forgot" to acknowledge his wife's birthday for the fourth year in a row. However, with Christmas approaching, he had to decide whether it was worth missing the family Christmas celebration in order to avoid seeing Julie.

Giving people the silent treatment is difficult, especially when they are part of our daily lives. We cannot ignore their physical presence. Giving God the silent treatment is easier. Because God does not have a physical presence that demands our attention, we can go weeks without speaking to God and maybe not even notice.

When distance grows between us and God, how do we repair that relationship? What will it take for us to notice how far we have wandered away from God?

Desolate

What a disaster! Not one, not two, but four great swarms of locusts had swept through Israel at the time Joel prophesied. Any grain that had been harvested and stored was devoured. The crops were eaten down to the ground. Grapevines that had been tended faithfully for decades disappeared in a flash. The grass and scrub plants that the livestock grazed on were utterly demolished. An invading army could not have done more damage than the locusts. It looked like the land had been scorched by fire for miles around.

The initial shock and devastation gave way to dread: What would the people eat now? What would the livestock eat? Were there even seeds left to plant for next year? How would the people live until next year with nothing to eat? It must have felt like the end of the world.

Perhaps we tend to overuse the word *disaster* these days. My child misses the bus to school on picture day? It is a disaster! All the frosting melts off the back of my wedding cake? What a disaster! I spill tomato sauce on my blouse right before heading to church? Disaster!

Of course, none of these things is a disaster. It may feel like the end of the world to be late, to appear disheveled, or not to have everything go perfectly smoothly; but each of these might someday make a funny story with enough time and distance. True disasters entail a loss that cannot be easily overcome with a little creativity or a sense of humor. We can continue to recall the horror of true disasters even at a great distance.

Not all of us have known disaster, but some of us have. Some of us have experienced catastrophic loss. It feels like the end of the world because it *is* the end of the world we thought we knew. The ground shifts beneath our feet, and we find ourselves gasping for air. How will we go on? Is survival even possible? "It stirs up great fear—who can endure it?" (Joel 2:11).

Then again, many of us have had times when we were pushed beyond what we thought we could endure. For instance, an accumulation of small mishaps and missed deadlines can become overwhelming when taken together. For others of us, even one small deviation from our expectations might have felt disastrous at times. When things that would appear trivial to other people do feel like the end of the world, it may be time to find help from a trained mental health professional.

According to the Depression and Bipolar Support Alliance, more than six percent of the adults in the United States are suffering from depression in any given year. Major depression does not just make "trivial" concerns *seem* catastrophic. Depression can have catastrophic results for those who suffer from it, as well as for their families and other loved ones, ranging from job loss to an increased rate of broken bones and other accidents to addiction and even death. Other mental illnesses have similar impacts on an ability to cope with day-to-day life. Perhaps many more of us are personally familiar with disaster than we let on.

What disasters face your community, your state, your country, or the world this week?

Disgraced

The people of Israel felt disgraced because the locusts were a sign from God that they had been disobedient. They felt as ashamed as a child punished in front of a classroom of peers.

Why do disasters happen? The Bible does not have just one answer for why bad things happen. It has many different answers. Prophets such as Amos and Micah warned of disasters that would come as punishments for a disobedient nation. Joel stood in this tradition. While he did not list specific sins that may have caused the destructive locusts to come, he did imply that the people's suffering was a punishment, a direct result of their disobedience.

In Joel 2:12-14, Joel told the people that God was "ready to forgive." If the people would repent, then this disaster could end and even be overcome.

However, even if this particular plague of locusts was a punishment, the Bible gives us examples of other reasons why people might suffer. A disaster is not a sure sign of God's wrath.

In the book that bears his name, when Job suffered a series of terrible misfortunes, his friends told him that he must have done something wrong in order to suffer so much. They begged Job to repent. Job repeatedly insisted on his innocence until, finally, God spoke up in Job's defense, confirming that Job was not being punished. It seems that Job suffered precisely because he was so righteous. God was testing him.

John 9 tells the story of Jesus and his disciples encountering a man who had been blind for his whole life. "His disciples asked him, 'Rabbi, who sinned, this man or his parents, that he was born blind?' Jesus answered, 'Neither this man nor his parents sinned; he was born blind so that God's works might be revealed in him'" (John 9:2-3, New Revised Standard Version). Then Jesus healed the man, giving him sight for the first time in his life. What was significant about this man's suffering was its eventual relief and the way in which this miraculous healing revealed God's power made manifest in Jesus.

Every disaster is a unique instance of human suffering. Even two seemingly similar disasters may have different causes. Many times, the Bible reminds us, we have no idea why suffering happens. In Luke 13:1-5,

Jesus told of two recent tragedies when many people lost their lives and said plainly that the individuals who died were not more sinful than anyone else, but he did not then give a substitute reason for why they died. We do not always have the answers.

Ecclesiastes reminds us that whatever the manner or the timing, we all die in the end. Trying to find the meaning in tragedy is often "pointless: the righteous get what the wicked deserve, and the wicked get what the righteous deserve" (Ecclesiastes 8:14). Ecclesiastes suggests that the better course is to simply enjoy good days when we have them and not ask too many questions about the bad days.

That is easier said than done, of course. It may be human nature to try to find the reason for tragedy. Consider "rubbernecking": When people see a car accident on the side of the road, they slow down, trying to discover what happened. Was it avoidable? Who was at fault?

At times, we may feel embarrassed by our misfortune because it is obvious that it arose from our own bad behavior in some way. Many times, however, we may feel embarrassed by our misfortune even though what happened is not our fault or is, in any case, a punishment that far outweighs our "crime." This feeling of having been disgraced can isolate us from others in our community and even from God.

Sometimes, people turn away from God in a time of crisis. Could it be that they feel they do not deserve God's love or help, are they afraid of drawing God's attention, or do they suppose that maybe God is not there for them anymore?

Is misfortune a sign that God is displeased with us?

Beloved

The locusts had eaten the grain offerings right out of the Temple! How could God have let this happen? Were the locusts more powerful than God? Where was God? Maybe there was no God. The people of God were beyond distressed.

When terrible things happen, it may feel like God is nowhere to be found. We may feel abandoned by the God who felt so near to us at other times. We may even find ourselves doubting whether God ever existed. Surely, if there was a God who loved us, these terrible things would not be happening.

The prophet Joel assured the people that they were still loved, that God loved them and would provide for them. God had pity on them, Joel said, and would perform signs to demonstrate that he was still with them and had not abandoned them (Joel 2:18-20).

Sometimes we need this reminder, too. Sometimes we need someone else to have faith in God's love for us when we are having trouble believing in it ourselves. At times, nothing may be able to persuade us of God's love, but we cannot ignore or deny the concrete love of another person for us. This is one of the many blessings of life in Christian community. God's compassion can reach us through others as our sisters and brothers in Christ lovingly tend to our needs.

Ultimately, however, our relationship with God is predicated on God's unending loving care for us. In order to mend or deepen our relationship with God, we need first to feel that there is someone there to relate to. We must "return to the LORD" (verse 13), or at least turn toward God, in order to rekindle our faith.

Joel reminds us that even when things are at their worst, God is trustworthy and ever-present. No matter what happens to us, Joel says, we can be assured that God's love is steadfast. God will be there for us when we return.

Are there times when it has been particularly difficult to believe that God loves you?

Repentant

No matter what the reason, any shift in our lives is an opportunity to turn to God. When we are shaken by something, this provides an opening for our relationship with God to shift, too.

Taking advantage of this opportunity requires keeping the lines of communication open. Sharing our thoughts and feelings with God is important, but it can be painful. Especially if we have not done it in a long time or if we are afraid that there is no one there listening to us or if we are afraid that the God who hears us is a God who is angry at us. It may feel easier not to bother.

We might try to escape from our suffering in many different ways. Some of these escapes can harm us or other people. Others appear fairly harmless: What does it hurt to turn on the television, pick up a magazine, go shopping, or talk on the phone? These things may be "godsends" in the way that they can help us get through the day when we are in crisis, but they also fill up spaces that we might use instead to talk with God.

Instead, we can use these very escapes as reminders of the God who is patiently waiting for us. Perhaps we can begin by simply acknowledging that God is there: "I'm sorry, God, I don't feel like talking to you right now, so I am turning on the TV instead." Or before calling a friend we might say, "I haven't heard you speak to me in a long time, God. If you have something to say to me today, will you say it through my friend or some other person I encounter today?"

We cannot begin to repair a relationship until we notice that it needs repairing. Whatever it is that causes us to notice a gap in our relationship with God—whether it is a disaster or not—that noticing is an opportunity. Simply seeing that we want our relationship with God to be different is a gift, a chance to come closer to the God who loves us so much.

How has your relationship with God changed over time? Can you identify particular events in your life that provided occasions for turning points?

Reliable God, you have told us that you will always be with us. This is so difficult for us to understand. Sometimes it seems that nothing much important is happening, and it is easy to forget you are there. Other times it is almost impossible to believe you are with us. Are you here and loving us when terrible things happen to us? Even when we don't understand you, God, help us to keep talking to you. Help us to keep believing that you love us and will care for us, no matter what happens; in Jesus' name. Amen.

Daily Bible Study

March 27	God's People Seek a Resting Place	Numbers 10:29-36
March 28	God the True Shepherd	Ezekiel 34:11-16
March 29	The Lord Brings the People Home	Jeremiah 23:1-8
March 30	Jesus Sacrifices for the Flock	John 10:11-18
March 31	Shepherds in God's Household Today	Hebrews 13:17, 20-21
April 1	Tending the Flock of God	1 Peter 5:1-11
April 2	A Caring Shepherd and Gracious Host	Psalm 23

God as Our Shepherd

Purpose

To claim what it means to trust God

Hearing the Word

Psalm 23
[1]The LORD is my shepherd.
I lack nothing.
[2]He lets me rest in grassy meadows;
he leads me to restful waters;
[3]he keeps me alive.
He guides me in proper paths
for the sake of his good name.
[4]Even when I walk through the darkest valley,
I fear no danger because you are with me.
Your rod and your staff—
they protect me.
[5]You set a table for me
right in front of my enemies.
You bathe my head in oil;
my cup is so full it spills over!
[6]Yes, goodness and faithful love
will pursue me all the days of my life,
and I will live in the LORD's house
as long as I live.

Key Verse: The LORD is my shepherd. / I lack nothing. (Psalm 23:1)

Seeing the Need

Along with a small group of friends, I was on the way to the airport in a foreign country when someone smashed the window of our van, grabbed my backpack off of my lap, and ran. One of my friends screamed, and I began to shake and cry. Then another friend leaned her head against mine and prayed, "Our Father, who art in heaven. . . . ." The familiar words were calming.

When she prayed, "Forgive us our trespasses, as we forgive those who trespass against us," I heard the words in a new way. My backpack was important—it had my passport in it, for starters, but even more important was the salvation of myself, my friends, the person who had taken my bag, and the police officers I would file a report with. Hearing those familiar words at a confusing and upsetting time reminded me of what I believed.

Perhaps you have had a similar experience at a funeral with Psalm 23: familiar words reminding you of what you believe in the midst of a confusing and upsetting time. We have heard these words so many times. Is it possible to hear them in a new way? No matter how familiar it is to us, this psalm has still more to teach us about what it means to trust God.

Living the Faith

The Valley of the Shadow of Death

Today, we are most likely to hear Psalm 23 at funerals. Often, all the mourners are invited to say the words of the psalm together, in the familiar words of the King James Version: "Yea, though I walk through the valley of the shadow of death" (verse 4).

Death can be a shock. Someone who was here just yesterday is gone today. One of the hardest things about the death of my father was when I would forget briefly that he was gone. I would get excited about calling him to talk about some new idea or experience before remembering that I could not call him anymore. You may have experienced something like this.

Perhaps, instead, you have lost someone who you felt had already been absent for a long time, the person you once knew lost through severe mental illness or dementia or through estrangement. Still, that person's death may have felt like a new loss, the loss of a possibility for reconciliation or the loss of the new person he or she had become that you had not realized you would miss.

Sometimes, we might perceive the death of a loved one as a blessing, for instance after a long and painful illness. Often, however, knowing that that person's death ended his or her suffering does not keep us from missing the person.

The death of someone close to us can feel frightening. We may be frightened of how our life is going to change without our loved one there for emotional or material support. This person we relied on was alive, and now he or she is not.

We may be surprised to find ourselves anticipating our own death, too. We may feel a bit frightened by the reminder that we, too, will undergo this mysterious transformation. We will cross the threshold from this life into death and into eternity, and none of our beloved friends and family may cross through with us. We will leave them behind, even as our loved one has now left us behind. The loneliness of this thought may feel frightening.

As we say the words, "I will fear no evil: for thou art with me" (verse 4, KJV), we remember what we believe: God is with us, even when it seems we are most alone. God is with us, even in our grief. God is with us, even in our death.

When is it most difficult to trust in God?

In Green Pastures

When have you especially noticed God's presence? God is with us all the time. Sometimes it is difficult to believe that God is there, but other times God's nearness may seem unmistakable.

There may be particular parts of worship when you feel God close to you: when you sing a particular hymn, receive Communion, or when the Scripture provides the very words you most need to hear. Maybe you have felt God with you just before you fell asleep or perhaps when you were standing in a field listening to the birds sing just before sunrise. Maybe God has come close to you when you were rocking a sleeping baby or stirring soup on the stove.

Some moments seem to be made for hearing God's breath and feeling God's embrace. These moments may stir us to laugh or cry or burst out singing, "He's got the whole world in his hands!"

This is one way to understand what it means to "rest in grassy meadows" (verse 2; "lie down in green pastures," KJV). Spiritually nourished by the moment, we can rest contentedly and simply enjoy the goodness of God. The King James Version continues in verse 3: "He restoreth my soul." Moments like these certainly do recharge our spiritual batteries! We can draw on the energy they give us to get us through spiritually dry times. Memories of having felt the divine presence can remind us that God is with us at other times when we feel more distant from God or maybe even have difficulty believing God is there.

This is important, because no matter how close we may feel to God at times, we face other moments when God is not in our view. We are easily distracted, and (like sheep) it is easy to let our eyes stray from our Shepherd. We can lose sight of God even if we attend church every week and make time for prayer every day. It might seem that weeks go by when we just catch glimpses of where God is headed. We may have "soul restoring" moments a couple of times a day for a week or more and then feel as if we are just going through the motions for months at a time.

However, going through the motions is not an empty gesture. When we remember the times we have felt God close to us, we are affirming that God's presence is real. When we go back to the places where we have seen God before, we are demonstrating our trust that God will show up again.

Instead of the words "he restoreth my soul" (verse 3), the Common English Bible reads, "he keeps me alive." These words may seem less strong, but they remind me that I can trust that God is with me, guiding me in the way to go, even when I am not having an earth-shatteringly spiritual experience. Sometimes, it might feel like you are just plodding along in the wilderness, and it takes a real effort to go back down to "the restful waters." While it is a great joy to be aware of God's presence in the moment, often we notice only in hindsight the many ways in which God was tending to us and feeding us all along.

What experiences have strengthened your trust in God?

The Lord Is My Shepherd

Like many psalms, Psalm 23 is written from the perspective of an individual. Instead of "The LORD is *our* shepherd" we read "The LORD is *my* shepherd" (italics added). We live and worship together as one body of Christ. Our faith is something that we do together, but our faith is also something that we do as individuals. Each of us has a faith that changes from day to day, from season to season. My body, my living situation, the church I attend, the job I am doing, the current experiences of my friends and family members—all of these things (and many more) make a difference in the way I experience God.

There are things I can do that will help me to grow in my trust in God. There are even things I can do that may support other people as they grow in their trust in God; but no matter how much I might want to be able to do so, I cannot make another person trust in God.

This can be frustrating for some of us. When we see people struggling and grieving, wondering where God is and why they are having so much trouble, it may seem obvious to us that they just need to trust in God. We might be tempted to share our opinion that they would not be struggling so much if they would just give in and trust in God.

Often, however, others to whom we might want to say this are those whose hearts are not ready for that message. When people feel like their lives are falling apart, God may feel untrustworthy to them. We may feel convinced that God is still taking care of them; but no matter how great our own faith is, we can make mistakes if we try to point out to other people the particular ways that God is at work in their suffering. We may guess in our hearts, but we cannot know for certain everything God is doing in other people's lives. We do not even know every way God is at work in us!

How can we support those who are having difficulty trusting in God without saying something that might lead them to trust God even less than they did before? Focusing on ourselves and our own trust in God may be a good first step. This may seem selfish, but Jesus reminds us in the Sermon on the Mount that we cannot see others clearly enough to help them until we first "take the log out of [our] eye" (Matthew 7:5). As our own trust in God increases, our need to know why each particular event happens as it does may decrease.

Trusting God to hear our prayers, we can pray for the people in our lives who do not trust in God in the same ways that we do. Praying for our own trust in God to increase, we may in time find ourselves relieved of the burdens of needing to know things only God can know and needing to save people only God can save. Our growing trust in God can free us to be simply lovingly present for people who are having trouble trusting in God.

When have you struggled to trust in God? How were Christian friends helpful or unhelpful in recovering your trust in God?

I Shall Not Want

"The LORD is my shepherd," our key verse reads and then continues, "I lack nothing." How many of us can say that and mean it?

Many of us feel that we lack something. Some of our desires may seem trivial. Janis Joplin mocked material acquisitiveness and the general dissatisfaction with life that fuels (and yet is not satisfied by) the quest for more stuff when she sang a song called "Mercedes Benz." However, rich or poor or in between, each of us has experienced non-trivial lack in our lives.

For instance, we may feel dissatisfied with our bodies for not working as well as we would like. When our health keeps us from doing things for our friends and family or even from taking care of ourselves, how can we say that we lack nothing?

Another person might have longed for a child and not been given one. How can we expect that person to say that they lack nothing? To say nothing of someone who lacks the bare essentials of life: enough healthy food, for instance, or a place to sleep that is safe, warm, and dry. How does that person say honestly, "I lack nothing"?

It may seem that the familiar King James translation provides us an answer here with the words "I shall not want." Perhaps it is our desires that we are supposed to reject. As a parent, one of my jobs has been to try to help my daughter differentiate between wants and needs. However, the meaning of the word *want* when the King James translation was made is fairly represented by the word *lack*. The old nursery rhyme that cautions "For want of a nail, the shoe was lost" does not imply that the problem was that the shoe desired a nail but that a nail was needed to hold the horseshoe in place. Similarly, "I shall not want" means for us today "I need [or lack] nothing."

There is more than one way to think about this. We can focus on the big picture or focus on what we do have instead of what we do not have or consider that we have been given all that we need for our salvation. For myself, some days I find it helpful to begin with the assertion that God is a trustworthy Shepherd, and therefore it must be true that "I lack nothing," however my life may appear to me at the moment. Then I ponder how that might be true.

To be honest, though, there are other times when asserting that "I lack nothing" is too hard for me to say with integrity, and I confess to God that I am having trouble believing that I have everything I need. God is trustworthy in all things. We can even trust God to continue to love us and listen to us when we are having difficulty trusting in God's providential care.

Are there things that you lack in your life? In what way is it true for you to say, "I lack nothing"?

Loving God, you are a trustworthy provider and protector. Even when our eyes are not on you, your eyes are always on us. You know us inside and out. Teach us to trust you more and more, and bring us back to you when we lose our way; in Jesus' name. Amen.

Daily Bible Study

April 3	God's Salvation Is for the World	John 3:17-21
April 4	Don't Love the World's Things	1 John 2:15-17
April 5	Nicodemus Pleads, "Give Jesus a Hearing"	John 7:45-52
April 6	The Serpent in the Wilderness	Numbers 21:4-9
April 7	Nicodemus Brings Spices for Burial	John 19:38-42
April 8	Rebirth and Renewal by Water and Spirit	Titus 3:1-7
April 9	God's Saving Love in Christ	John 3:1-16

God's Saving Love in Christ

Purpose

To understand Jesus as the incarnate expression of God's love

Hearing the Word

The Scripture for this lesson is printed below. The background text is John 3:1-21.

John 3:1-16
[1]There was a Pharisee named Nicodemus, a Jewish leader. [2]He came to Jesus at night and said to him, "Rabbi, we know that you are a teacher who has come from God, for no one could do these miraculous signs that you do unless God is with him."

[3]Jesus answered, "I assure you, unless someone is born anew, it's not possible to see God's kingdom."

[4]Nicodemus asked, "How is it possible for an adult to be born? It's impossible to enter the mother's womb for a second time and be born, isn't it?"

[5]Jesus answered, "I assure you, unless someone is born of water and the Spirit, it's not possible to enter God's kingdom. [6]Whatever is born of the flesh is flesh, and whatever is born of the Spirit is spirit. [7]Don't be surprised that I said to you, 'You must be born anew.' [8]God's Spirit blows wherever it wishes. You hear its sound,

but you don't know where it comes from or where it is going. It's the same with everyone who is born of the Spirit."

[9]Nicodemus said, "How are these things possible?"

[10]"Jesus answered, "You are a teacher of Israel and you don't know these things? [11]I assure you that we speak about what we know and testify about what we have seen, but you don't receive our testimony. [12]If I have told you about earthly things and you don't believe, how will you believe if I tell you about heavenly things? [13]No one has gone up to heaven except the one who came down from heaven, the Human One. [14]Just as Moses lifted up the snake in the wilderness, so must the Human One be lifted up [15]so that everyone who believes in him will have eternal life. [16]God so loved the world that he gave his only Son, so that everyone who believes in him won't perish but will have eternal life.

Key Verse: God so loved the world that he gave his only Son, so that everyone who believes in him won't perish, but will have eternal life. (John 3:16)

Seeing the Need

"Hosanna!" the people cried, waving palm branches and laying their robes in the street to create a royal carpet for Jesus' donkey to tread on. They believed in Jesus, but what did they believe?

Their belief quickly turned to doubt when Pilate brought Jesus before them days later, arrested and bound. Who was Jesus? Perhaps he was nothing more than an agitator who had pushed the Romans too far. Better to be on the side of the ones with the long spears than on the side of the one whose hands were tied. "Crucify him!"

Today, the idea of Jesus' crucifixion is less distressing to us in some ways. Unlike the crowds on Good Friday, we know the rest of the story. The Resurrection is, among many other things, a vindication that Jesus is who he said he was—God with us—but do we live as if Jesus is who he said he was? Or do our beliefs quickly turn to doubt when following Jesus gets dangerous or confusing?

Who is Jesus? What does it mean to believe in him? Nicodemus may not have known he was asking these questions, but Jesus heard his questions and gave Nicodemus life-giving answers.

The Temple

The Temple in Jerusalem was the seat of Jewish religious power, but from the beginning, it had a kind of political power as well. As a place of obligatory pilgrimage, the Temple in Jerusalem was the place people went to encounter God through the proxy of the Temple priests who governed all access to God.

Jesus was performing signs in Jerusalem, and he was operating outside of the approved channels for encountering God. In this way, he was reminiscent of the earliest Hebrew prophets, such as Elijah and Elisha. As someone familiar with the Scriptures and traditions of Judaism, Nicodemus recognized the parallels between Jesus and the Hebrew prophets; he recognized that Jesus was a messenger from God. The prophets often found themselves dangerously in conflict with the powers that be, which Nicodemus would also have recognized. This may be why he came to Jesus at night.

John records Jesus as putting himself into conflict with the Temple at the beginning of his ministry. Just before today's passage, we can read John's account of Jesus driving the merchants and moneychangers out of the Temple (John 2:13-17). The other Gospels remember this event as taking place on Palm Sunday, in the last week of Jesus' earthly life. They remember this as one of the provocations that led to Jesus' crucifixion.

For John, however, it seems that this claim of authority within and over the Temple is an important clue to who Jesus is, important enough to place this story near the beginning of his Gospel. Jesus was acting on God's behalf, within the place that claimed to hold God's presence. The Temple was meant to be a house of prayer, where people could meet God, but people were acting for their own gain in that place, without fear of God; and Jesus made it clear that it was unacceptable to use God's name in such a cynical way.

As important as the Temple was, it could not contain God. "God's Spirit blows wherever it wishes," Jesus told Nicodemus (John 3:8). God is free to act in whatever way he chooses and is free even to choose to appear within the constraints of a human life, which is what God was, in fact, doing in Jesus.

God entered the Temple as the Son Incarnate, expressed his dissatisfaction with what was happening there, and walked out again. Jesus did not need anyone to testify about him, to understand and speak accurately about what he was doing, in order for the work he was doing to be effective. In fact, no one yet did seem to understand that he was something more than a prophet and a miracle worker. God in God's freedom was doing something brand new.

In what ways does God behave in predictable ways? In what ways is God unpredictable?

Jerusalem

Today is Palm Sunday, when we celebrate Jesus' triumphal entry into Jerusalem. Many churches now also anticipate Good Friday on this Sunday. The combined Palm/Passion Sunday reminds us that many who were in the crowd welcoming Jesus to Jerusalem still did not understand who Jesus was. When he was arrested later that week, many of his followers turned on him. Even his own disciples ran away. Jerusalem was the city that welcomed Jesus as king—and the same city of people who cried, "Crucify him!"

Soon after the miracle of turning water into wine at the wedding at Cana, Jesus went to Jerusalem to celebrate the Passover, the same festival that was being celebrated at the time of his crucifixion. People were excited about the miracles that Jesus was performing, but the Gospel tells us, "But Jesus on his part would not entrust himself to them . . . for he himself knew what was in everyone" (John 2:24-25, NRSV).

What did he know about the people who "believed in his name" in Jerusalem? Among many other things, I imagine Jesus knew that they did not know who he was. They did not understand the purpose of his ministry.

Nicodemus went to Jesus seeking understanding. At first glance, it appears that Nicodemus had Jesus all figured out. After all, the first thing he said after approaching Jesus was, "Rabbi, we know that you are a teacher who has come from God" (3:2). Why bother going to Jesus at all, then? He spoke with the safe distance provided by the word "we," but he went to Jesus alone.

Nicodemus was not looking for a debate or for his witty repartee with Jesus to be noticed by the right people. He was looking to learn something more. Given Jesus' answer to him, it seems that Jesus perceived that what Nicodemus wanted was to see God.

Living in the Holy City of Jerusalem was not, after all, all that different from living in any other city. People had to work and cook and eat and sleep as they would in any other city. People cared for one another and argued with one another as they would in any other city. Roman soldiers were stationed in Jerusalem just as they were in cities throughout the Mediterranean at that time.

Studying the Scriptures, worshiping in the Temple, living in the Holy City of Jerusalem—none of these things had been enough for Nicodemus to give him the vision of God's kingdom that he craved. However, then he saw Jesus. God was clearly doing something in Jesus! So Nicodemus went to him. He did not know what to ask, exactly, but Jesus, who saw into everyone's heart, knew Nicodemus was hungry for God.

If Nicodemus was going to see the kingdom of God, he was going to need to be ready to see with new eyes, to listen with new ears, to understand with a new mind. God was doing something new. Jerusalem was not the center of God's revelation. Jesus was.

Are you hungry for God? What ideas or commitments might God be asking you to sacrifice in order to put Jesus in the center of your life?

Israel

"How is it possible for an adult to be born?" Nicodemus asked indignantly. "It's impossible to enter the mother's womb for a second time and be born, isn't it?" (John 3:4). He had come for help, and this rabbi was talking in riddles.

"You are a teacher of Israel and you don't know these things?" Jesus countered (verse 10). Why does Jesus sound impatient here? Perhaps he was frustrated that Nicodemus was struggling with concepts found throughout the Hebrew Scriptures.

For instance, Exodus points to God's freedom when God told Moses, "I will be gracious to whom I will be gracious" (Exodus 33:19, NRSV). Isaiah tells of God's promise to act in new ways: "See, the former things have come to pass, / and new things I now declare" (Isaiah 42:9, NRSV). Even the words of the psalmist anticipate Jesus' teaching about being born again: "Create in me a clean heart, O God, / and put a new and right spirit within me" (Psalm 51:10, NRSV).

Nicodemus was right to call Jesus "Rabbi." Jesus was intimately familiar with the Hebrew Scriptures, and he referred to those Scriptures when he taught others about God's love. His mother was a faithful Jew who trusted in God so deeply that she humbly accepted God's plan for her, saying, "I am the Lord's servant" (Luke 1:38). When Jesus spoke to people about entrusting themselves completely to God, he spoke out of the rich religious tradition of Judaism and out of his own experience growing up with people who had acted in faith and hope that God acted through and in the lives of the Jewish people.

Not everything Jesus had to say was easily derived from the Old Testament, however. He had new information about himself and his place in God's plan. "If I have told you about earthly things and you don't believe, how will you believe if I tell you about heavenly things?" he asked Nicodemus (John 3:12).

If Nicodemus was resisting the ideas of God's freedom and the need to be born again—ideas that had clear antecedents in the Hebrew Scriptures—then how was he going to take the news that Jesus was the Savior of the world? God was doing something new, and Nicodemus had not even absorbed "the former things" that had "come to pass."

Unlike many Jewish believers living today, Nicodemus (and others in the Israel of Jesus' day) had lost sight of the radical freedom of God. How could they accept the good news of Jesus as the incarnate expression of God's love if they believed that God was predictable? How could Jesus help Jews like Nicodemus grow into Jews like his mother Mary, believers who would say yes to a new and radical plan to bring God's love to the world?

While Jesus certainly had a mission to the entire world, that mission began with a mission to the Jewish people. He interacted with many Gentiles, but he spent nearly his entire life in areas where the majority of the population consisted of fellow Jews. His adult ministry, as recorded in the Gospels, took place in an area about the size of the state of Connecticut. It would be up to his followers to take the good news of who Jesus was to the rest of the world.

What stumbling blocks have made it difficult for you to understand Jesus as God with us?

The World

"God so loved *the world*" (John 3:16, italics added). The concentric circles of the Temple, Jerusalem, and Israel determine the context of our reading, but Jesus was God's expression of love for the whole world. God saw that all people—not just the Jewish people—were lost in darkness. They did not know that God loved them. God sent Jesus into the world as a light.

In the dark night of this world, where things can seem so uncertain, the love of God in Jesus cuts through the darkness like the beam of a lighthouse, showing ships which waters are safe and which are unsafe, saving them from running aground or even from death.

The purpose of Jesus coming into the world was to be the embodiment of God's love. The purpose was not condemnation (verse 17)—everyone was already in the dark, on the outside of God's saving love. Jesus came as God with us, as a sign of how far God would go to include us in that saving love, and as an invitation to become not strangers, nor even servants, but friends (15:15). Jesus came to overcome sin and death, to conquer everything that would keep us apart from God. However, by refusing God's love in Jesus, we might remain as condemned as we were already. We might choose to remain in the dark.

Just because God sent Jesus into the world to save the world does not mean that the mission has been accomplished just yet. "The light came into the world, and people loved darkness more than the light, for their actions are evil" (3:19). We remember this today in worship, how quickly the cries of "Hosanna!" turned into cries of "Crucify!" However, Nicodemus did not abandon Jesus, even in death. He had come to see Jesus in a new way. He had, it seems, been born anew (19:38-42).

God's love is for every person. Jesus demonstrated this care in the variety of people he reached out to: young and old, Jew and Roman, male and female. He touched people no one else would touch and spoke to people no one else would speak to. He ate with notorious sinners and with respected religious teachers alike. Jesus' life and ministry make it clear that God's love is for all people—even for Nicodemus, even for us.

As Jesus' modern-day disciples, it is our mission to carry this news into the world that God so loved. May we live in a way that is inspired by our faith in Jesus. May we extend to every person we encounter the love that God has extended to us, in the sureness that God's love and forgiveness are available to them, no matter who they are.

Astonishing God, in your freedom you choose to act in ways we never could imagine. Yet your every action is consistent with your love for us and for the entire world. Thank you for the gift of your Son, Jesus, whose life, death, and resurrection brought us our salvation; in Jesus' name. Amen.

Daily Bible Study

April 10	Jesus' Side Is Pierced	John 19:31-37
April 11	The Spirit, Water, and Blood Agree	1 John 5:6-12
April 12	The Lord Breaks No Bones	Psalm 34:15-20
April 13	Soldiers Cast Lots for Jesus' Clothing	John 19:24 (or 25)
April 14	Jesus' Final Words to His Mother	John 19:26-27
April 15	The Women and Peter Were Amazed	Luke 24:1-12
April 16	Victory Over Death	John 20:1-10; 1 Peter 1:3-5, 8-9

God's Love as Victory Over Death

Purpose

To celebrate that God's love cannot be defeated!

Hearing the Word

The Scripture for this lesson is printed below. The background texts are John 19:38-42; 20:1-10; 1 Peter 1:3-9.

John 20:1-10

[1]Early in the morning of the first day of the week, while it was still dark, Mary Magdalene came to the tomb and saw that the stone had been taken away from the tomb. [2]She ran to Simon Peter and the other disciple, the one whom Jesus loved, and said, "They have taken the Lord from the tomb, and we don't know where they've put him." [3]Peter and the other disciple left to go to the tomb. [4]They were running together, but the other disciple ran faster than Peter and was the first to arrive at the tomb. [5]Bending down to take a look, he saw the linen cloths lying there, but he didn't go in. [6]Following him, Simon Peter entered the tomb and saw the linen cloths lying there. [7]He also saw the face cloth that had been on Jesus' head. It wasn't with the other clothes but was folded up in its own place.

[8]Then the other disciple, the one who arrived at the tomb first, also went inside. He saw and believed. [9]They didn't yet understand the scripture that Jesus must rise from the dead. [10]Then the disciples returned to the place where they were staying.

1 Peter 1:3-5, 8-9
[3]May the God and Father of our Lord Jesus Christ be blessed! On account of his vast mercy, he has given us new birth. You have been born anew into a living hope through the resurrection of Jesus Christ from the dead. [4]You have a pure and enduring inheritance that cannot perish—an inheritance that is presently kept safe in heaven for you. [5]Through his faithfulness, you are guarded by God's power so that you can receive the salvation he is ready to reveal in the last time. . . .

[8]Although you've never seen him, you love him. Even though you don't see him now, you trust him and so rejoice with a glorious joy that is too much for words. [9]You are receiving the goal of your faith: your salvation.

Key Verse: Then the other disciple, the one who arrived at the tomb first, also went inside. He saw and believed. (John 20:8)

Seeing the Need

When Bill woke up, he saw his 16-year-old granddaughter, Elena, sitting next to his hospital bed. She quickly wiped her eyes with her sleeve. "You can't fool me, Ellie," Bill said. "Why are you crying?"

"Oh, Grandpa. I don't want you to die!"

"Well, until Jesus comes back, everyone's got to die. But I'm not scared because I know that death is not the end of the story. God's love is with me wherever I go, even in death."

"But it's the end of *our* story. God gets to stay with you, but I don't. And I'm going to miss you!"

Elena rested her head on Bill's shoulder and began to cry again. He stroked her hair like he used to do when she was a baby and whispered, "I don't have all the answers, Ellie. But I believe that God is the one who wrote our story and that it is a story about the God who loves you and me and everyone. God loves you even more than I do, and God will give you everything you need."

In a world in which each of us continues to suffer, what does it mean to say that God's love cannot be defeated? Even if we do not have all the answers, we can still trust in God's unstoppable love.

Living the Faith

Joseph and Nicodemus

John's Gospel tells us that Joseph of Arimathea was a secret follower of Jesus (John 19:38). He was afraid of being found out because Jesus was seen as a troublemaker by the Jewish leaders, and perhaps Joseph did not want to lose whatever influence and power he had with his people. Maybe he was just afraid of looking like a fool, following an itinerant preacher from Galilee, or perhaps he was even afraid for his life.

Nicodemus had been afraid, too. He had come to Jesus only at night the first time (3:2). We never learn if he continued meeting with Jesus or if he just returned to his daily life while quietly thinking about all that Jesus had said on that one strange night.

In any case, Nicodemus and Joseph now had nothing to lose. The authorities had taken care of their problem with Jesus and his followers. Jesus had been arrested, sentenced, and executed. Jesus was no longer a threat to anyone. No one could fault Joseph and Nicodemus for a devout good deed: caring for the dead body of a poor Jew from out of town (19:38-42).

When the sun sets on Friday, all work is forbidden to devout Jews, and Jesus and his followers were all devout Jews. Jesus' crucifixion on a Friday presented a difficulty: The body had to be dealt with before the sun went down, but they had not been expecting this to happen. Jesus was supposed to be the Messiah! Surely, he would overcome the Romans at the last minute! Now they had a scant couple of hours to prepare the body, and no one had the necessary materials.

No one except for Joseph and Nicodemus. When did Nicodemus purchase the 75 pounds of myrrh and aloes? Had he bought it when he heard that the authorities were plotting against Jesus or when Judas was recruited by the authorities to betray Jesus? Did he buy it on Friday morning when

Jesus was brought before Pilate? Perhaps he waited until the cross was lifted into place on Golgotha. Nicodemus having the necessary materials to tend to Jesus' body suggests that he was expecting the story to end this way. Jesus was going to die, and someone was going to have to tend to the body.

Similarly, I get the impression that Joseph of Arimathea was prepared. He had probably thought it out beforehand: "If Jesus gets killed in Jerusalem, then I am going to go ask for the body. I have a tomb all ready for him." While Jesus' other followers were still reeling from the shock of his death, Joseph and Nicodemus were taking the necessary steps to tend to Jesus' dead body. It makes me wonder if they were less in shock than the other followers if they had been expecting something like this all along.

Joseph and Nicodemus were followers of Jesus. They believed that Jesus was on God's side, but perhaps they did not believe that that was going to make enough of a difference. Time after time in Roman-occupied Judea, they had seen the forces of Rome overcoming wisdom, truth, and love. Why should Jesus be any different?

When has it been difficult for you to believe in the power of God's love?

Mary Magdalene

For many more of Jesus' followers, however, it had not seemed possible that Jesus would die—certainly not so soon after riding in triumph into the city, with everyone waving palm branches! Jerusalem was his for the taking, and as the Chosen One of God, it was his by right. How could Jesus be dead?

Everything had happened so fast. Praise God, Nicodemus and Joseph had been prepared, but they had been in such a hurry. Could they have possibly done everything correctly? Had they left anything undone?

Mary could not be sure. She had to go check up on their work. She had to see Jesus' body and satisfy herself that everything necessary had been done for him. It seems likely that Mary had believed that Jesus was going to inaugurate God's reign in Jerusalem, that she had recognized in Jesus the truest embodiment of God's love she had ever seen, and that she believed that there was no way he could be defeated by anyone.

However, even if she had been wrong about Jesus—even though Jesus had died—she still loved him. Even if Jesus was not the Messiah, even if Jesus was just an ordinary person, he was her friend. He was everyone's friend, or at least he was a friend to anyone who would accept his friendship. Mary owed it to such a beloved teacher and friend to make sure he had a proper burial.

When she reached the tomb, however, she "saw that the stone had been taken away" (John 20:1). The tomb was opened! The body was gone! Had it been stolen? Had somebody moved it? Perhaps she was at the wrong tomb. What could have happened?

It did not occur to Mary yet that Jesus could have risen from the dead. Death was final. She was confused and upset and was going to need help thinking this through. She went to her friends for help.

Think of a time when God did not do what you had expected. How did you cope? Did your ideas about God change?

Peter and the Other Disciple

Jesus' disciples were still in disbelief. I wonder what they were talking about when Mary came running into the room, talking about Jesus' missing body (John 20:2). Certainly, they were not sitting around waiting for Jesus to appear. Many had seen him die, including "the disciple whom [Jesus] loved" (19:25-30). John's Gospel is clear that "they didn't yet understand the scripture that Jesus must rise from the dead" (20:9).

Maybe they were trying to decide what to do next, now that Jesus had not turned out to be who they had thought he was. Perhaps they were wondering if now the Romans were going to crucify them, too; or maybe they were too sad and shocked to have any thought for themselves at all. Whatever they had been thinking, they had not gone with Mary to the tomb. There was no point in it. Jesus was dead, and life as they had known it was over.

Now Mary was among them saying that Jesus' body had been taken. Who knew what fresh insult was going to be added to the injury of his loss? Peter and another disciple leaped up and ran to the tomb. They had to see for themselves.

What they saw was not, strictly speaking, an empty tomb. Jesus' body was no longer there, but his grave clothes were (verses 5-7). Peter noticed them and probably wondered about them. It did not make sense that someone would go to all the trouble of removing a body from the grave clothes before stealing it. Was there no ready explanation, miraculous or otherwise, that entered his mind? The body was gone; that much was certain. Mary had been right.

Today we read in John's Gospel that the other disciple saw the tomb and the empty grave clothes "and believed" (verse 8); but what did he believe, I wonder? After all, the next verse was about them not understanding that the Scriptures said that Jesus would rise from the dead!

Was his belief specific? Did he believe that Jesus had been resurrected, or was his belief more general than that? Did he believe that there had been some sort of miracle, and he did not know what it was; or did he believe something different than what had happened, that Jesus' body had been taken up to heaven, maybe?

Whatever he believed, the other disciple did not understand, any more than Peter did, that the Resurrection was necessary or that it had been foretold. He may not have understood the significance of Jesus' resurrection or even that it had happened at all. That would come later. (The "yet" in "they did not yet understand" implies that they did eventually come to understand.) However, he believed something. His faith in Jesus was returning. God had done something special through the Resurrection to signify how special Jesus was. Something unusual had happened, and God had done it.

What have you "seen and believed"? Can you think of something you witnessed that you were convinced could only be explained by God's intervention?

Ourselves

Gradually, Jesus' followers came to understand that he had been bodily resurrected. Taken together with the evidence of his missing body, Jesus' many post-burial appearances could not be explained any other way. They were amazed, strengthened, and convinced that they had to share this news with all the world. The news of Jesus' resurrection has been passed from person to person across generations, and so it has reached us. This is how it is that we have learned to love Jesus without ever having seen him (1 Peter 1:8).

This means that our experience of the Resurrection is different for us than it was for Jesus' first followers. From the beginning, we learned the story of Jesus' death and resurrection as one story. We did not have to cope with the massive grief and disappointment of Jesus' public execution as it unfolded. Instead, with our distance from those events, the Resurrection can seem to us like an obvious necessity.

Of course, Jesus could not stay dead! How could God incarnate be defeated by death? God is Lord of all—even over death! Furthermore, God had promised to defeat death on our behalf. As Isaiah foretold: "He will swallow up death forever" (Isaiah 25:8, NRSV). There was no other way for the story to go. Jesus had to be resurrected.

God's love for us was embodied in Jesus, who lived 2,000 years ago in a small province in the Eastern Mediterranean. What an astonishing miracle that we could have been embraced by God's love so far away and long ago! However, God's love is stronger than anything—stronger than distance, stronger than the flow of time, stronger even than death. Death could not have the final word.

In the Resurrection, we learn that God's love cannot be defeated because it is stronger than anything else. This is our "pure and enduring inheritance" (1 Peter 1:4): God's powerful love, God's promise to be faithful, which nothing can sweep aside.

This can be hard to reconcile with a world in which there is still suffering and death, a world in which people still hurt one another on purpose. How can we affirm that God's love cannot be defeated without failing to acknowledge those whose lives have been dominated by degradation and abuse?

Like "the other disciple," there are things we believe without understanding all of the details. We believe that Jesus rose on Easter morning and that he will reign over an unending kingdom of light and love, but sometimes we do not understand why we are still waiting for his return.

We believe that God's love is stronger than any other power in the universe, but sometimes we do not understand why God chooses to intervene to right some wrongs and not others. We believe that God has called us to be agents of love in the world, but sometimes we do not understand why it continues to be so hard for us to know and to do God's will.

Sometimes our lack of understanding overwhelms us, and we begin to have doubts. On other days, we find that we are able to celebrate all of the wonderful truths we know about God without needing to understand every detail because we know that God is trustworthy. When we remember and trust in God's steadfast love for us, when we believe it in our hearts, we "rejoice with a glorious joy that is too much for words" (1 Peter 1:8).

Jesus Christ is risen! He is risen indeed!

What is something that you believe without understanding certain details?

Astonishing God, your love is stronger than anything we can imagine. Just when we think there is no way that love can prevail, you intervene in ways we could not expect. By resurrecting Jesus, you showed us that even death cannot come between us and your love. Thank you for the gift of your amazing, unstoppable love; in Jesus' name. Amen.

Daily Bible Study

April 17	Mutually Sharing the Gospel of Christ	Romans 1:1-15
April 18	Fruit of Justification by Faith	Romans 5:1-5
April 19	Grace Abounded Through Jesus Christ	Romans 5:18-21
April 20	Believers' Present Suffering and Future Glory	Romans 8:18-25
April 21	God's Will Shapes Human Direction	Romans 8:26-30
April 22	Paul's Faithful Ministry Despite Suffering	2 Corinthians 11:21-27
April 23	God's Love Never Changes	Romans 5:6-11; 8:31-39

God's Reconciling Love

Purpose

To live with the confidence that God loves us at all times and in all circumstances

Hearing the Word

The Scripture for this lesson is printed below. The background texts are Romans 5:1-11; 8:31-39.

Romans 5:6-11

[6]While we were still weak, at the right moment, Christ died for ungodly people. [7]It isn't often that someone will die for a righteous person, though maybe someone might dare to die for a good person. [8]But God shows his love for us, because while we were still sinners Christ died for us. [9]So, now that we have been made righteous by his blood, we can be even more certain that we will be saved from God's wrath through him. [10]If we were reconciled to God through the death of his Son while we were still enemies, now that we have been reconciled, how much more certain is it that we will be saved by his life? [11]And not only that: we even take pride in God through our Lord Jesus Christ, the one through whom we now have a restored relationship with God.

Romans 8:31-39

[31]So what are we going to say about these things? If God is for us, who is against us? [32]He didn't spare his own Son but gave him up for us all. Won't he also freely give us all things with him?

[33]Who will bring a charge against God's elect people? It is God who acquits them. [34]Who is going to convict them? It is Christ Jesus who died, even more, who was raised, and who also is at God's right side. It is Christ Jesus who also pleads our case for us.

[35]Who will separate us from Christ's love? Will we be separated by trouble, or distress, or harassment, or famine, or nakedness, or danger, or sword? [36]As it is written,
We are being put to death all day long for your sake.
We are treated like sheep for slaughter.

[37]But in all these things we win a sweeping victory through the one who loved us. [38]I'm convinced that nothing can separate us from God's love in Christ Jesus our Lord: not death or life, not angels or rulers, not present things or future things, not powers [39]or height or depth, or any other thing that is created.

Key Verses: I'm convinced that nothing can separate us from God's love in Christ Jesus our Lord: not death or life, not angels or rulers, not present things or future things, not powers or height or depth, or any other thing that is created. (Romans 8:38-39)

Seeing the Need

Darius had been making the produce delivery a couple of times a week for years now, and he always took a few minutes to talk with Ernie, the restaurant manager. This week, Ernie told Darius that he had to go to court to work out a new child support plan. As he so often did, Darius promised to pray for Ernie.

"What makes you think God cares what happens to me?" Ernie asked. "I cheated on my wife, I probably drink too much, and I don't go to church."

Darius looked thoughtful. "I've always been taught that God loves you no matter what. But since you mention church, you want to come with me? I know you work Sunday mornings, but we have a Sunday night Bible study."

"Me? At church? I'm not sure I even believe in God."

"God believes in you whether you believe in God or not. What do you have to lose?"

Darius hoped Ernie would go to church with him, but even more, he hoped Ernie would notice that nothing he said scared off Darius.

Who is welcome in your church? Are there people who might be received only reluctantly? What (if anything) could disqualify a person from having God's love made available to them? Paul reminds us, "Christ died for ungodly people" (Romans 5:6).

Living the Faith

Neither Death Nor Life

In today's key verse, Paul offers reassurances, listing all the many things that cannot separate us from the love of God. He begins his list with "death." Death will not separate us from God's love. Christ defeated death, and we now have "the hope of God's glory" (Romans 5:2). As we discussed in last week's lesson, God's love is stronger than anything, even death.

Even though this is a central tenet of our faith, death is sufficiently mysterious and seemingly final, so it is obvious why we might need reassurance that death would not separate us from God's love. It is interesting, however, that Paul goes on to tell us that life will not separate us from God's love either! This is intriguing: How would life separate us from God?

Certainly, "death or life" (8:38) is a compelling poetic pair, but I do not think the word "life" appears here just because it sounds good. I think Paul meant for us to understand "life" as a category of a created thing that can seem to be a threat to God's love for us.

Life can present us with all sorts of distractions and obligations that can make it more difficult for us to follow God. While we are taking care of our bodies, our possessions, our homes, and our loved ones, we can lose sight of God; but God never loses sight of us.

In the 300's A.D., some Christians waited to be baptized until they were on their deathbeds. They thought that if baptism was for washing away their sins, a single sin after being baptized would be enough to consign them to hell. Life being complicated and risky, it was impossible to commit to possibly decades of never sinning, so they waited until they were safely stuck in bed and days or hours from death before receiving baptism—their one and only "get out of jail free card." They did not want life to separate them from the love of God.

This is a fairly accurate view of sin. Even with the best intentions, we have so many occasions to sin in each day that we are bound to fall prey to one or two of them. However, it is not a helpful view of baptism, and it is not a view that seems to account for God's boundless love.

Paul writes, "If we were reconciled to God through the death of his Son while we were still enemies, now that we have been reconciled, how much more certain is it that we will be saved by his life?" (5:10). God's love and forgiveness are not available to us just one time, in our baptism. God's love and forgiveness are available to us at all times throughout our lives—before our baptism, in our baptism, and after we are baptized, as well. Life cannot separate us from God's love.

When has life and its circumstances made you feel as though you were disconnected from God?

Neither Angels nor Rulers

When I was in kindergarten, I was erroneously punished for something another child did. I do not remember the circumstances now, but I remember my feelings of fear as I stood in the corner. How could my teacher not know I would not have done something like that? Would my teacher call my parents, and would they believe her? To be sure, I legitimately misbehaved on occasion and needed punishment, but having a trusted authority figure make a mistake about me was devastating.

I imagine being misrepresented or misunderstood is an experience many of us share. Charles Albert Tindley wrote about a similar experience in the popular hymn "Stand by Me": "When I've done the best I can, and my friends misunderstand, / thou who knowest all about me, stand by me" (*The United Methodist Hymnal*, 512). Paul assures us that God will indeed stand by us in every time of trial, even in the last judgment (Romans 8:33-34).

God is not persuaded by the arguments any other person might make against us. Nothing another person says or does can make God stop loving us. God is more powerful than any other person. This power extends to loving us more than any other person can love us and knowing us better than any other person can know us. No matter what anyone else might say, God has the final say. Other human beings, even other Christians, may try to place us outside of God's saving love, but God is the one who loves us and who advocates for us.

No person's opinions can stand between us and God's love. This can be tremendously empowering, enabling people of faith to stand up for what is right. In his "Letter From Birmingham Jail," Martin Luther King Jr. wrote to the many church leaders who stood opposed to the Civil Rights Movement.

King and those who worked with him were not swayed by other people's opinions that the problems of racism were not serious enough to justify the "extreme" measures of boycotts and marches and that black Americans simply needed to wait patiently for better treatment, which would surely materialize by and by. The women and men who fought for the safety and dignity of black Americans were less concerned about what others thought of them than whether they were embodying the truth of God's love for all people.

Has an authority figure ever failed you?

Neither Present Things nor Future Things nor Powers

Paul is clear in his conviction that nothing happening now, nor anything that will ever happen, can stand in the way of God loving us. Sometimes, however, things may happen that stand in the way of us trusting in God's love.

In 2004, on the day after Christmas, a massive earthquake in the Indian Ocean triggered tsunamis in 14 countries, killing and displacing so many people that an exact count is impossible. Over 200,000 people lost their lives. Many people around the world wondered, *If God loves us, why would God let such a terrible thing happen?* A person did not have to have ever been to Indonesia or another affected country in order to grieve the sudden loss of whole communities.

For other people, a crisis of faith may arise from a tragedy closer to home. Seeing someone we love suffer from a terrible disease and having our prayers for their release seemingly go unanswered can leave us wondering, "Where are you, God? Do you love us?"

Paul suffered greatly in the course of his life, and yet he was "convinced that nothing can separate us from God's love" (Romans 8:38). Trusting in God was what made it possible for Paul to endure suffering. Instead of his suffering defining how he saw God, Paul's vision of God defined how he saw his suffering. Any trouble he experienced was transitory compared to a never-ending life in harmony with God (Romans 8:18, 21).

It is not easy to wait through difficult and painful times for the glory of God to be revealed. Paul used the image of a woman in labor (8:22) to describe the feeling of waiting for God's love to be fully expressed in the world. Thinking about that metaphor, it seems to me that our suffering is not any less because of the great joy that God promises is on its way, nor is our patience with the pain necessarily any greater; but we can endure it when we remember that God has a miraculous new creation on the other side of our suffering.

When has suffering (your own or someone else's) made it difficult to trust in God's love? How (if at all) has trusting in God's love made a difference in your ability to endure suffering?

Neither Height nor Depth

One of my favorite Scriptures is Psalm 139. Paul's assurance that neither height nor depth can separate us from the love of God reminds me of verses 7-10 of that psalm. Like the psalmist, Paul reminds us that wherever we might go, God is already there. You may think that this is obvious. Of course, God is everywhere, but it can be easy for us to forget, especially if we have gotten into the habit of thinking of ourselves as carrying God with us.

God is in places where we have never been and sees into the hearts of other people whom we have never met. It is true that wherever we go, God goes with us. We carry our knowledge and assurance of God's love with us wherever we go, but that love is also already in a place before we ever get there.

This is a reason to celebrate! Wherever we go, there is a chance that we may see divine love already at work, if we look for it. As we go about God's work in the world, God is working on us, too, transforming our hearts and eyes and ears to be more and more like God's. We are invited to be part of taking the good news of a new creation to people who are not aware of how much God loves them. We are also given opportunities to witness that love at work in ourselves and other people in ways that further transform and expand our own understanding of God's love.

In the story with which we began our lesson, I wonder what Ernie might learn from Darius and his friends if he ever makes it to Sunday night Bible study, but I also wonder what Darius and the other people at his church might learn from Ernie. All along, God has been in Ernie's restaurant, Ernie's house, the family court where Ernie will hear the ruling about the child support he owes. God has been with Ernie everywhere he has gone, even though he has not realized it. I wonder what Ernie will be able to share about the places where he has already encountered God's love once he begins to recognize God's presence in his life.

Are there places where you have felt particularly assured of God's loving presence? Are there places where you have struggled to see God?

God, our dearest Friend and our mighty Creator, it is amazing that you can be so huge and powerful and yet so lovingly concerned with every detail of our lives. Sometimes we get distracted and forget where you are or even who you are. Thank you for always loving us, even when we are not paying attention, and for giving us so many reminders of your love in your Scriptures, in other people, in every place and every time; in Jesus' name. Amen.

Daily Bible Study

God's Preserving Love

Purpose

To recognize and respond to Jesus' loving leadership

Hearing the Word

John 10:1-15

[1]I assure you that whoever doesn't enter into the sheep pen through the gate but climbs over the wall is a thief and an outlaw. [2]The one who enters through the gate is the shepherd of the sheep. [3]The guard at the gate opens the gate for him, and the sheep listen to his voice. He calls his own sheep by name and leads them out. [4]Whenever he has gathered all of his sheep, he goes before them and they follow him, because they know his voice. [5]They won't follow a stranger but will run away because they don't know the stranger's voice." [6]Those who heard Jesus use this analogy didn't understand what he was saying.

[7]So Jesus spoke again, "I assure you that I am the gate of the sheep. [8]All who came before me were thieves and outlaws, but the sheep didn't listen to them. [9]I am the gate. Whoever enters through me will be saved. They will come in and go out and find pasture. [10]The thief enters only to steal, kill, and destroy. I came so that they could have life—indeed, so that they could live life to the fullest.

[11]"I am the good shepherd. The good shepherd lays down his life for the sheep. [12]When the hired hand sees the wolf coming, he leaves the sheep and runs away. That's because he isn't the shepherd; the sheep aren't really his. So the wolf attacks the sheep and scatters them. [13]He's only a hired hand and the sheep don't matter to him. [14]"I am the good shepherd. I know my own sheep and they know me, [15]just as the Father knows me and I know the Father. I give up my life for the sheep.

Key Verses: I am the good shepherd. I know my own sheep and they know me, just as the Father knows me and I know the Father. I give up my life for the sheep. (John 10:14-15)

Seeing the Need

Has a friend or family member ever told you, "Jesus told me to. . . ."? Has a church leader ever said to you, "Jesus wants you to. . . ."? Did you wonder how they knew it was Jesus who was leading them and not some other impulse?

As Christians, our desire to please Jesus can make us particularly susceptible to listening to someone who will tell us what Jesus wants us to do, but Jesus himself warned that not everyone who used his name was doing so sincerely (for example, Matthew 7:15-23). So how can we tell the difference between people who are cynically using Jesus' name to manipulate us, people who sincerely but wrongly believe that Jesus has given them a message, and people who have heard a word from the Lord? Should we just reject anything anyone says about "Jesus told me. . . ."? What if they are right?

Christians can affirm that by the power of the Holy Spirit, Jesus continues to provide leadership for us today. Recognizing what Jesus is calling us to do and where Jesus is calling us to go can be difficult sometimes, but God has provided us with many tools for hearing Jesus rightly.

Living the Faith

One Shepherd or Many Shepherds?

The Hebrew people were a pastoral people. From the beginning, the patriarchs were nomadic herders of sheep and goats. When Joseph's family settled in Egypt, they identified themselves as shepherds. When

Moses fled Egypt, he fled to Midian, itself a herding culture. Centuries later, tending livestock (and sheep in particular) still dominated Hebrew life.

Perhaps it is because of this familiarity with sheep and with the care they require that the person of the shepherd is a common metaphor for care and leadership throughout the Hebrew Bible. For instance, David was a shepherd before he became the king of Israel, and he famously described God as a shepherd (for instance, in Psalm 23, which we discussed in Lesson 5, as well as in Psalm 28:9).

The prophets continually returned to the image of a shepherd to talk about the failings of the leaders of Israel and Judah. Like shepherds tending sheep, the kings and priests were supposed to tend to the people, but, instead, they failed the people. They were supposed to care for those in their charge, but they cared only for themselves. Instead of being good shepherds, they were bad shepherds, misleading the people and abandoning them to predators.

In this context, Jeremiah and Ezekiel foretold a good shepherd God would anoint to lead the people (Jeremiah 23:1-6; Ezekiel 34). When Jesus called himself "the good shepherd" (John 10:14), he was identifying himself with an image of Messianic leadership established in the Hebrew Scriptures. He was telling those who had ears to hear that he was the One God had sent to rescue and to lead the people.

As he did so many other times, Jesus took traditional language and used it to say something new. Whereas the Hebrew prophets and others had used the word *shepherd* to describe any leader of the Jewish people, Jesus insisted that he was the only Shepherd. Other human leaders were not failed shepherds but "hired [hands]" (verses 12-13). Only so much could be expected from them because they were not invested in the sheep. Only the owner of the sheep was the true shepherd; only the one who owned the sheep could care for the sheep in a total way.

Calling other human leaders "shepherds" implied an ownership of the people that Jesus rejected. In some sense, didn't the person ruling at the time "own" the people? No. Jesus was saying that neither the Roman governor nor King Herod nor the chief priest was anything more than a representative at best. They did not own the people. Only God owned the people. Anyone else who claimed ownership of another person or group of people was a thief and an outlaw (verse 8).

Jesus' words echo the psalmist's words: "Know that the LORD is God— / he made us; we belong to him. / We are his people, / the sheep of his own pasture" (Psalm 100:3). God's ownership of humanity, and of all the world, was rooted in creation (Psalm 24:1-2).

This means that Jesus' saying "I am the good shepherd" only makes sense when we understand Jesus as God incarnate. If God alone owned the people, then only Jesus—fully God and fully human—could be a human leader deserving of the title *shepherd*.

God is so much greater than anything we can comprehend. We are more unlike God than sheep are unlike a shepherd. At times, we can no better understand God's intentions than sheep can understand a shepherd. Sheep know that they can trust the shepherd who provides for them—provides food, water, shelter, and protection. In the same way, recalling creation reminds us that God has provided us with everything we need. God has even provided us with our very selves. We can trust in the loving guidance that God offers us in Jesus.

How is the idea of God's "ownership" of you comforting? In what ways is the idea uncomfortable?

One Voice or Many Voices?

Today, one of the words we use for leaders in the church is *pastor*, which is directly borrowed from the Latin word for "shepherd." However, pastors understand that they are not the One Shepherd of their congregations. They are leading on God's behalf. Pastors do not lead on their own authority. They need God's guidance to lead the people.

How do pastors and other Christians receive God's guidance? When Jesus is not physically among us, how can we today claim to hear his voice? Are we like sheep without a shepherd? How can we know with clarity where Jesus is leading us? We may wish we were like people who lived in Jesus' day who could see and touch Jesus in person and hear his words directly; but Jesus promised, "I won't leave you as orphans" (John 14:18). By the help of the Holy Spirit, Jesus continues to lead us today.

One way we hear Jesus speaking to us today is in his words and teachings that have been passed down to us. In some churches, the people in the congregation stand up when the Gospel lesson is read in worship. We can imagine that this signifies that we are paying special attention to these words spoken by and about Jesus. We remember that Jesus promised "the Holy Spirit . . . will remind you of everything I told you" (14:26).

The Scriptures as a whole are God's gift to the church. Many people make Bible reading part of their prayer time. They reflect on what they read and ask God's help in understanding it. Reading the Scriptures can be part of our conversation with God, one of the ways that Jesus speaks to us. However, different parts of the Scriptures can sometimes appear to be saying different things, and Christians can sometimes even read and pray over the same passage of Scripture and get different ideas about what it means and what Jesus would have them do.

While the Bible is a gift from God, the Bible is not itself God. When we read the Scriptures, we hear the voices of God's faithful followers through the centuries. Through them, we may hear the voice of Jesus. How can we tell when we are hearing Jesus, the Living Word, through the words on the page?

When have you felt you were hearing Jesus speak to you through the Scriptures?

One Body or Many Bodies?

Matthew records Jesus as saying, "For where two or three are gathered in my name, I am there among them" (Matthew 18:20, NRSV). Paul expanded on this idea with his idea of "the body of Christ." He told the Corinthians, "You [plural] are the body of Christ and parts of each other" (1 Corinthians 12:27). In this way, we can imagine that if the community of all Christians is the body of Christ, then we can hear the voice of Jesus when we are in community with our fellow Christians.

Paul illustrated his understanding of the body of Christ with the Eucharist: "Isn't the loaf of bread that we break a sharing in the body of Christ? Since there is one loaf of bread, we who are many are one body, because we all share the one loaf of bread" (1 Corinthians 10:16-17). As Christians, we share a common worship life, which forms our understanding of what it means to follow Jesus.

When we are in conversation with our brothers and sisters in Christ, we can listen for Jesus' voice. No one of us is the body of Christ all by ourselves, and in the same way, no one Christian can speak for Jesus all by himself or herself. However, in our life together, formed by baptism, by Holy Communion, by the Bible, and by prayer, we find common ground in which to speak to one another where we believe God to be at work and where we believe God to be leading us.

Christians may (and do) disagree about what they hear Jesus saying to their communities. This would seem to contradict the idea that we can hear Jesus through prayerfully consulting with other Christians. What we hear will depend on whom we ask, won't it? If we cannot count on our faith communities to speak with a single voice on some issues, why should we trust what they have to say about anything at all?

Perhaps we are most confused about what Jesus is saying when we try to figure out what he is saying to everyone about a big issue all at the same time. However, when we ask more focused questions for ourselves ("What should I do about . . . ? Should I go do . . . ?"), we may hear Jesus answering us through holy conversations, and Jesus' voice may sound clearer to us in that moment than we ever thought possible.

What makes a conversation a "holy conversation"?

One Shepherd, Many Sheep

Perhaps the most important part of hearing Jesus' voice is being willing to hear his voice. In the verse from Psalm 100 about God being the one who owns us, quoted above, some ancient versions of this psalm add "and not we ourselves," as in, we do not own ourselves. Neither are we our own shepherds.

If we are searching the Scriptures for evidence of what we expect or want to hear, then we are not listening for Jesus' voice. If we only listen to Christian friends who agree with us and not to those who disagree, then we are not listening for Jesus' voice.

This is not an excuse to bully Christians who disagree with us, telling them that if they do not listen to our voice, then they are not listening to Jesus. On the contrary, if (as Paul reminds us in Corinthians 13) "love is patient" (1 Corinthians 13:4), then we can be patient with our Christian friends who disagree with us. If "love doesn't keep a record of complaints" (1 Corinthians 13:5), then we can continue to hope for reconciliation, and we can all admit with Paul that "now I know partially" (1 Corinthians 13:12).

Instead, recognizing that we are not shepherds to ourselves or anyone else frees every one of us to be ready to hear Jesus saying things that are uncomfortable for us. If we are only led where we were already inclined to go, then we do not need a leader at all.

We know that we do need Jesus to lead us and not only because there are so many others who are ready and willing to lead. The wolves in sheep's clothing that Jesus warns about in Matthew 7:15 are the thieves and outlaws of John 10. "The thief enters only to steal, kill, and destroy," Jesus says in John 10:10, continuing by contrasting this with his own loving leadership, which completes the work of God's good creation: "I came so that they could have life—indeed, so that they could live life to the fullest."

This is one way that we can test if the voice we hear is Jesus' voice: Does the voice speak destruction in our life? Does it tear us down and make us doubt God's love, or does the voice give life?

Jesus came so that we might have life—abundant life, life rooted in God's love for us and for all creation. When Jesus leads, we may not end up where we intended, but we can be sure we will arrive in a place where we need to be. When Jesus speaks, he may not say what we expected, but we can be sure that his words will be life-giving.

Can you think of a time when Jesus' words were life-giving for you?

Our Creator, you made us and we are yours. Thank you for giving us Jesus' loving leadership. Without Jesus, we would be lost. Open our ears that we might hear Jesus speaking to us clearly. Open our hearts, that we might desire to go wherever he leads us; in Jesus' name. Amen.

Daily Bible Study

May	1	God Knows Where I Am	Psalm 139:1-6
May	2	Can I Flee From God's Presence?	Psalm 139:7-12
May	3	The Lord's Voice in the Storm	Psalm 29:1-9
May	4	Compassion After Rejection	Isaiah 54:1-10
May	5	God's Wrath Against Nineveh	Nahum 1:1-8
May	6	Fleeing From God's Call	Jonah 1:1-6
May	7	God's Sustaining Love Despite Rebellion	Jonah 1:7-17

God's Sustaining Love

Purpose

To rejoice that God can transform even our misdeeds into an opportunity to demonstrate loving care for others

Hearing the Word

The Scripture for this lesson is printed below. The background text is Jonah 1.

Jonah 1:7-17

[7]Meanwhile, the sailors said to each other, "Come on, let's cast lots so that we might learn who is to blame for this evil that's happening to us." They cast lots, and the lot fell on Jonah. [8]So they said to him, "Tell us, since you're the cause of this evil happening to us: What do you do and where are you from? What's your country and of what people are you?"

[9]He said to them, "I'm a Hebrew. I worship the LORD, the God of heaven—who made the sea and the dry land."

[10]Then the men were terrified and said to him, "What have you done?" (The men knew that Jonah was fleeing from the LORD, because he had told them.)

¹¹They said to him, "What will we do about you so that the sea will become calm around us?" (The sea was continuing to rage.)

¹²He said to them, "Pick me up and hurl me into the sea! Then the sea will become calm around you. I know it's my fault that this great storm has come upon you."

¹³The men rowed to reach dry land, but they couldn't manage it because the sea continued to rage against them. ¹⁴So they called on the LORD, saying, "Please, LORD, don't let us perish on account of this man's life, and don't blame us for innocent blood! You are the LORD: whatever you want, you can do." ¹⁵Then they picked up Jonah and hurled him into the sea, and the sea ceased its raging. ¹⁶The men worshipped the LORD with a profound reverence; they offered a sacrifice to the LORD and made solemn promises.

¹⁷Meanwhile, the LORD provided a great fish to swallow Jonah. Jonah was in the belly of the fish for three days and three nights.

Key Verse: Then the men were terrified, and said to him, "What have you done?" (Jonah 1:10)

Seeing the Need

Joan went to church, but her sister, Leslie, did not. Leslie had not felt comfortable around "those people" since her release from prison. Instead, she said TV was her church. She loved to watch one preacher in particular.

Joan called her brother to complain. "Buck, she has given that man money again and again. He has his own plane, and she has a trailer with no air conditioning. He's just using God's love to take people's money. It isn't right!"

"You're right," Buck replied. "But it seems to me that the preacher isn't the only problem here. Some folks at church are choosing to judge Leslie, and Leslie is choosing to hide at home watching TV. I'm just glad she's hearing about God's love and forgiveness from someone. Once she really believes that for herself, maybe she'll have the strength to face people who know where she's been."

Joan was not satisfied with that answer. She was glad, too, that Leslie was showing some interest in God, but she wanted the preacher who was making so much money off of people like her sister to face some consequences.

Can God reach people when we testify to him, no matter what our intentions are? If so, do our intentions matter?

God's love is so powerful that even our bad behavior cannot stand in its way. However, we are still accountable for our sins, even when God uses them to reach out in love to other people.

Living the Faith

"I Worship the LORD"

Have you ever heard of an "elevator speech"? This concept comes from the modern world of business. An elevator speech is a 20-30 second prepared speech pitching what is essential for someone to know about you and your project, whether you are looking for a job, trying to sell a product, or hoping for financial backing for your business idea.

Some Christians have developed their own versions of the elevator speech to talk about Jesus—a 20- or 30-second response they have memorized for when the opportunity comes to share their faith with other people.

Like any marketing tool, elevator speeches can come in handy; and like any marketing tool, elevator speeches can ring false if they become disconnected from who we actually are and what we actually believe. However, in that moment, the Holy Spirit can assist us in finding the words to speak that are true about Jesus as well as true to ourselves and our experience as children of God (Luke 21:13-15, NRSV).

Writing an elevator speech about Jesus can be a good exercise for us. It can help us think about what we believe to be most important and most compelling about the Christian life. On the other hand, what we say spontaneously might better reflect the truth of the state of our relationship with God in the moment and leaves room for the Spirit to provide the words a person most needs to hear.

Wakened in the midst of a storm at sea, fleeing from his responsibility to God, Jonah did not have much he wanted to report about his relationship with God in the moment. So when the sailors asked Jonah who he was, Jonah fell back on what sounds like a prepared answer—an abbreviated elevator speech: "I'm a Hebrew. I worship the LORD, the God of Heaven—who made the sea and the dry land" (Jonah 1:9).

Jonah's speech was pithy. It expressed a great deal of important information in few words. (You can read it out loud in about five seconds.) However, this speech does not ring true. Jonah simply was not acting like someone who had taken his own words to heart. These sound more like words he had memorized than words that actually guided his life decisions.

After all, if Jonah's God was "the God of heaven" (the sky that stretches unbroken over every place in the world), and if God "made the sea and the dry land" (and so has mastery over those elements, too), then how exactly did Jonah propose to flee from this God (verse 3)? The sky stretched over Tarshish, too! Jonah remained in God's domain through every minute of his travel over the sea to the dry land of Tarshish.

While the ship's officer questioned how Jonah could sleep through such a rough storm, we might question how Jonah could sleep knowing that he had so brazenly disobeyed the God he was sworn to serve. He had heard God's word clearly; running away was not an accident. Jonah could only have slept if he thought that he was in no danger.

Did Jonah think that it was possible for him to get away from God— that God was not actually the God of heaven but only God in Israel? Or did he think instead that God might not care all that much about his disobedience and would just find someone else to "go to Ninevah . . . and cry out against it" (verse 2)? Either way, his actions proved that it was no longer true that Jonah worshiped the Lord because he had chosen to stop paying attention to what God said and hoped God would just leave him alone.

Perhaps there was a time when Jonah believed the words in his speech. Perhaps he was sincere in his desire to serve the God of heaven once upon a time. It is clear, however, that by the time we enter Jonah's story, he no longer believed at least part of what he told the sailors about himself and God.

If you were writing an elevator speech about your faith in God, what would be most important to include?

"What Have You Done?"

Unlike Jonah, the sailors recognized right away what a foolish thing Jonah had done. As soon as Jonah described God, the sailors "were terrified and said to him, 'What have you done?' " (Jonah 1:10). Jonah had previously told them that he was running away from his God, but the sailors were familiar with many local gods. They had never imagined that Jonah might be running away from a God who was every-where, a God who had power over everything. Miraculously, instead of doubting Jonah's description of God, the sailors instead doubted Jonah's good sense in running away.

How did the sailors even get to the point of asking Jonah about himself? In verse 7, we learn "they cast lots, and the lot fell on Jonah." This, to the sailors, would have been a sure sign (from their gods, perhaps they imagined; from God, we would say) that Jonah knew something about the terrible storm, and maybe he even knew how to make the storm go away.

This storm was particularly bad. We know this because the sailors were scared (verse 5). Assuming that at least some of them were experienced sailors, they would have seen other storms before; they would have known better than anyone what constituted "normal" weather on the Mediterranean.

We also know this was an unusually bad storm because the sailors threw the cargo overboard (verse 5). The whole point of sea travel was to carry cargo from one port to the next; no one could stay in business long if throwing cargo overboard was a regular occurrence. It was an act of desperation. If praying with words was not enough, perhaps some sort of sacrifice was required. Better to lose only some cargo than lose the entire boat, cargo, people, and all.

The storm likely came on quite suddenly, as well. The sea had been quiet enough for Jonah to fall asleep in the hold; he was "deep in sleep" (verse 5). We do not know how many minutes or hours he was asleep before the storm blew in; but because people can be hardest to wake in the first few hours of sleep, we can imagine that the sea went from calm to terrifying relatively quickly. In other words, the sea was behaving unusually badly.

All of this was so out of the ordinary that the sailors began looking for a reason for it. By casting lots, they settled on Jonah as the reason (verse 7).

What Jonah told them was reason enough for a storm of this magnitude. The sailors asked Jonah, "What have you done?" (verse 10), but they knew exactly what he had done. Jonah had crossed "the God of heaven—who made the sea and the dry land" (verse 9). They asked in the way that a parent might ask a child, "What are you doing?" when they can see plainly that the child is scribbling on the wall. What the parent means is, "What are you thinking? Why are you doing this?"

Similarly, the sailors knew what Jonah had done; they just did not know why anyone would think to do it. Like incredulous parents, the sailors wanted to know, "What were you thinking?" How had Jonah thought that he could get away with it? How could he not have expected serious consequences when he ran away from God?

Like the child scribbling on a wall with a crayon, it is likely that Jonah simply had not been thinking about anything but what he wanted. He did not want to do what God had asked, and he behaved impulsively.

Most of us have probably not done anything as dramatic as boarding a boat for the end of the known world, but perhaps we all know what it is like to have acted rebelliously and impulsively. If we stopped to pray first, we know God would ask us to do something we do not want to do, so instead we turn our backs on God; and, like Jonah, we illogically hope God will not care or will not notice.

What one event or decision would you chose to revisit if you could go back in time and ask your younger self, "What are you doing?"

"Hurl Me Into the Sea!"

The biblical account reminds us at this point that "the sea continued to rage" (Jonah 1:13). Lest we forget, this was not a leisurely conversation about the nature of God and faith: Jonah and the sailors were talking about God in the midst of a terrifying storm. In fact, they were only talking about God because of the storm. Without the storm, Jonah would still be peacefully sleeping below the deck, and the sailors would be going about their business.

This was a practical conversation, so the sailors asked the next most logical question, "What will we do about you so that the sea will become calm around us?" (verse 11). Jonah answered dramatically, "Pick me up and hurl me into the sea!" (verse 12). The sailors must have been horrified. What Jonah was suggesting was murder. They tried to row back to dry land instead. Better to put Jonah off the boat in a place where he had a chance of surviving.

These sailors were ripe for conversion. They were basically decent people. Even though Jonah had endangered their lives, they attempted to save his life rather than throw him overboard as he had suggested. They had no compunction about sacrificing their own pay in the form of the cargo in order to save their lives and the lives of everyone on the ship; but they would not sacrifice even one selfish foreigner for the sake of everyone else, even with his consent (even urging), at least not until they had tried everything else.

They were also basically devout people. Their first impulse when facing the storm had been to pray, and they understood quickly what an error Jonah had made in running away if he was right in what he claimed for his god. They did not yet believe in the One God, but they understood the implications of such a god far better than God's own prophet did. Just one sentence of half-hearted testimony from Jonah in the right context was enough for them to consider the possibility that such a God existed.

One act of power attributed to this God would be enough to inspire them to worship and make vows to God. Jonah's last act of prophecy on the boat ensured that the sailors would understand that God was responsible for raising the storm and for ending it. God acted, but first Jonah predicted and defined God's deed of power: "Pick me up and hurl me into the sea! Then the sea will become calm around you" (verse 12), and it happened just as Jonah said.

It is difficult to know if this constituted Jonah taking responsibility enough to admit that if the lot had fallen on him and revealed that God had made this storm in response to Jonah getting on the boat, then the only solution was to remove Jonah from the boat with great haste. Was this a moment of repentance for Jonah, or was Jonah still trying to get away from God? Did he intend to die and so relieve himself of the responsibility of going to Nineveh? Whereas it is clear that getting on the boat was an act of faithlessness on the part of Jonah, it is less clear whether letting himself be thrown overboard was an act of faithfulness.

Jonah should not have been on that boat in the first place; but as long as he was there, in the wrong place, God could still use him to do something right. God could use Jonah's elevator speech. God could even use Jonah's despairing desire to be thrown to the bottom of the sea. The sailors would know that the God of the Hebrews was "the God of heaven—who made the sea and the dry land" (verse 9). They would learn about life lived in obedience to this God.

We all make mistakes. Sometimes, we are even willfully disobedient. We might not always behave in the way that God would like us to; but thanks be to God, there is nothing we can do that God cannot use for a good end.

"So what are we going to say? Should we continue sinning so grace will multiply? Absolutely not!" (Romans 6:1-2). This knowledge that God can make use of us even when we are misbehaving is not a license to sin. Instead, it is further evidence of the power of God's love. Even if we run in the opposite direction from where God would have us go, we cannot stand in the way of God's determination to share love with all people.

Have you ever heard God speak through an unlikely witness? Have you ever been an unlikely witness to God's love?

Loving God, our Creator and Friend, you made all things and see all things. We know that there is nowhere we can go that is apart from you, and yet sometimes we wish we could. We wish we could be carried away by our desires; we wish we could avoid people we do not wish to help. Have mercy on us, Lord. When we stray from you, remind us that we are still your children. Transform our misdeeds into acts of love and power, and turn us back to you. Keep us close, and fill us with the desire to serve you with gladness; in Jesus' name. Amen.

Daily Bible Study

May 8	Thanks for Deliverance From Death	Psalm 116:1-14
May 9	Who Can Be Safe With the Leviathan?	Job 41:1-11
May 10	The Lord Will Strike, Then Heal	Isaiah 19:19-22
May 11	Answer Me, O Lord	Psalm 69:13-18
May 12	Something Greater Than Jonah Is Here	Luke 11:29-32
May 13	Make Disciples of All Nations	Matthew 28:16-20
May 14	Jonah's Song of Thanksgiving	Jonah 2

God's Love Preserved Jonah

Purpose

To remember God's steadfast love for us, even when we have been disobedient

Hearing the Word

Jonah 2

[1]Jonah prayed to the LORD his God from the belly of the fish:
[2]"I called out to the LORD in my distress, and he answered me.
From the belly of the underworld I cried out for help;
you have heard my voice.
[3]You had cast me into the depths in the heart of the seas,
and the flood surrounds me.
All your strong waves and rushing water passed over me.
[4]So I said, 'I have been driven away from your sight.
Will I ever again look on your holy temple?
[5]Waters have grasped me to the point of death;
the deep surrounds me.
Seaweed is wrapped around my head
[6]at the base of the undersea mountains.
I have sunk down to the underworld;
its bars held me with no end in sight.
But you brought me out of the pit.'

[7]When my endurance was weakening,
I remembered the LORD,
and my prayer came to you,
to your holy temple.
[8]Those deceived by worthless things lose their chance for mercy.
[9]But me, I will offer a sacrifice to you with a voice of thanks.
That which I have promised, I will pay.
Deliverance belongs to the LORD!"
[10]Then the Lord spoke to the fish, and it vomited Jonah onto the dry land.

Key Verse: But me, I will offer a sacrifice to you with a voice of thanks. / That which I have promised, I will pay. / Deliverance belongs to the LORD! (Jonah 2:9)

Seeing the Need

For many months, Joe's favorite sports star had been denying taking performance-enhancing drugs. However, new evidence had arisen, and now this same star was confessing that he had used the drugs after all. "I'm sorry to have let down my fans," he said.

"You're only sorry you got caught!" Joe shouted at the TV in the break room, disgusted. The athlete had let him down. Joe had been defending him all along, and now he felt betrayed.

His coworker Nikki disagreed. "C'mon, Joe. He says he's sorry. We should believe him."

"Of course, he's sorry he 'let down his fans.' Now we aren't going to buy his merchandise anymore. Nothing he said sounded like he was actually sorry for what he did, about using the steroids."

Their friend Mira popped her head into the break room to see if Joe had heard the news. "He's heard all right," said Nikki, shaking her head.

Mira listened to Joe's complaints, then asked, "I wonder what will happen to him?"

"I don't know," Joe answered, "but he'd better not get off easy."

When someone does something wrong, we want them to be sorry, but what if they are not sorry? Will they "get what they deserve"?

God loves us even before we are sorry. Sometimes it may seem as if God is more patient with us than we deserve.

Living the Faith

What Does the Bible Say?

When reading Scriptures, some Bible scholars talk about our "hermeneutical lens" (hur-muh-*noo*-ti-kuhl), meaning an idea or a set of related ideas that we bring with us when we interact with the world and particularly when we read a biblical text. *Hermeneutic* means a way of interpreting things. *Lens* is added to remind us that we wear some of our ideas like glasses: We see the entire world through them.

A hermeneutical lens can be a good and helpful thing. For instance, it fills me with delight when I look at the world as the beloved creation of God, and I manage to treat people with more respect and consideration when I choose to see them as people for whom Jesus lived and died. I look through other lenses without even noticing I am doing it.

When talking about his congregations in England, a pastor friend of mine sometimes has to remind me, "That's how it works in churches in the Southern United States, but in British Methodism. . . ." I am always wearing my American glasses, and sometimes that makes it hard for me to stay focused on what my English friend is asking me to see.

Many Christians believe that each person's relationship with God is transactional, that God's forgiveness is only for people who are sorry for what they have done. These Christians read the Bible through "transactional glasses."

There are Bible passages that tell us that if we repent, God will forgive us. For instance, in words that many preachers will repeat as an invitation before the prayer of confession, we read in 1 John 1:9, "If we confess our sins, he who is faithful and just will forgive us our sins and cleanse us from all unrighteousness" (NRSV).

Will God forgive us only if we repent? If we are not sorry, does God not forgive us? Certainly, there are some places that seem to indicate that. In Romans 2:1-16, Paul warns his readers that it is dangerous to claim to follow God and not change their ways. Some Gospel passages warn that failing to forgive others prevents us from receiving God's forgiveness (Matthew 6:14-15; 18:21-35; Mark 11:25). This could be interpreted as our salvation being contingent on us repenting of our anger.

These and other Scriptures, together with some of the traditions of the church (represented in the words we speak in worship, the prayers of confession we pray, and the hymns we sing), are the substance of the transactional glasses many of us wear. Wearing these glasses makes us feel comfortable. It hardly seems fair if people can go on doing bad things without ever being sorry for them and receive forgiveness anyway. When we are wearing these glasses, everything we see and hear and read tells us "God is fair." The idea that God's forgiveness is only for people who ask for forgiveness is a core belief for many Christians.

However, wearing these glasses might make it harder to recognize when the Scriptures we are reading do not fit into this "repentance, then mercy" pattern. In many instances in the Bible, God gives people (and in other cases, nations) second chances without waiting for them to be sorry. Jonah 2 seems to be one of those places.

In my daughter's Bible, the notes on Chapter 2 say that God tells the fish to spit Jonah out onto the beach because Jonah had asked God's forgiveness for making the wrong choice. Look at Jonah 2 again closely. Read it in a number of different translations. Does it sound to you like Jonah was sorry about what he had done—or only sorry to have nearly drowned? (Maybe he was sorry to be stuck inside of a fish. It must have been dark and smelly in there.) When I read Chapter 2, the only thing I hear Jonah come close to expressing sorrow about is the possibility of never seeing the Temple again.

So why did that note in my daughter's Bible say Jonah asked God for forgiveness? Because the idea that God's mercy is only for people who ask for forgiveness is a core belief for many Christians, perhaps the writer of that note was so committed to that belief that it made it hard to see what was (and what was not) actually in the text. Maybe the writer did see that Jonah did not repent in Chapter 2 but thought that was not a good lesson for children and so decided to say something more acceptable, even if it meant inaccurately portraying the actual words of the Bible.

Even if we want the entire Bible to speak with one voice about something we care about, we still need to read each Scripture carefully. God may be saying something to us that we did not expect to hear.

What are some of your hermeneutical lenses? What ideas and identities are you looking through when you read the Bible?

What Does Jonah Say?

In the entire account of Jonah, Jonah only second-guessed his behavior once: in the last chapter, when he complained to God about the results of his obedience to God. Essentially, Jonah was sorry he had surrendered to God and obediently gone to Nineveh (Jonah 4:1-3). This is not the "right kind of sorry" for a follower of God to be.

In last week's lesson, we saw that Jonah admitted that the storm had been the result of his disobedience, and he (maybe) accepted the consequences. However, he never apologized to the sailors or to God.

Most of Chapter 2, the basis for this week's lesson, takes the form of a psalm, a prayer Jonah prayed while he was inside the big fish. It is a prayer of petition, a prayer of thanksgiving, and a bargaining prayer. At no point, however, is it a prayer of confession. Jonah did not admit to wrongdoing. He did not say he was sorry, and he did not ask for forgiveness.

Jonah began his prayer by describing his thoughts and feelings as he was sinking into the sea. As he sank, Jonah was afraid he was going to die, and he asked God to help. Might Jonah have been thanking God in advance for rescuing him from the inside of the fish? Perhaps, but it sounds more like he was thanking God for rescuing him from drowning. If God had not "provided a great fish to swallow Jonah" (1:17), he would indeed have drowned.

God's "holy temple"—that is, the Temple in Jerusalem—is mentioned twice in 2:2-9. In verse 4, Jonah piously wondered if he would ever see the Temple again. He did not seem so concerned about seeing the Temple when he was fleeing to Tarshish! However, after having a near-death experience and having been reminded of God's power, his first thought was of the Temple.

What does it mean that Jonah wanted to worship God in the Temple but was not interested in doing what God asked him to do? Other prophets, such as Amos, warned that God preferred obedience to worship in the Temple (Amos 5:21-24). Jonah's words are conventionally pious, but they do not demonstrate respect for what God wanted from him.

Later, in Jonah 2:7, Jonah's words suggest that the place where prayers are heard, no matter where they are offered, is in the Temple in Jerusalem. In this context, when Jonah offered to make a sacrifice to God, he most likely meant a sacrifice in the Temple in Jerusalem (as is meant throughout the psalms, such as in Psalm 66:13-15).

Did Jonah not learn anything from this episode? God had asked him to go to Nineveh. We might think that a natural response at this point in the story would be for Jonah to say, "I'm sorry, God. I see you were serious, and you really did want me to go to Nineveh. If it is not too late, I will do what you asked and go." However, this is not what Jonah said. Instead, what Jonah seems to have prayed was, "Thank you, God, for keeping me from drowning in the sea. If I ever get out of this fish, I'm going straight to Jerusalem to offer a proper thank-you in the Temple."

What makes a prayer a "good prayer"?

What Does God Say?

In the Hebrew Bible, Jonah 2 begins with the last verse of the Christian Old Testament's Chapter 1: "Meanwhile, the LORD provided a great fish to swallow Jonah. Jonah was in the belly of the fish for three days and three nights" (1:17). Reading Chapter 2 in this way provides context for Jonah's prayer. It also has the effect of giving God the first and the last word.

Read in this way, God rescues Jonah twice in Chapter 2: when God says no to allowing Jonah to drown by providing the fish and when God says no to allowing Jonah to be digested by the fish, instead causing the fish to vomit Jonah on the shore. God says yes to Jonah, miraculously saving him in spite of his rank disobedience.

Why not just let Jonah plummet to the sea floor and recruit someone else to go to Nineveh instead? Why did God give Jonah a second chance?

We do not know why God gave Jonah another chance to do the right thing. If we were in God's shoes, we might conclude that Jonah was a liability and try to find someone who would do the right thing without complaining. However, God did not do this. God "spoke to the fish" (verse 10), and the fish safely delivered Jonah to the shore.

Jonah did not simply "get away with it," either. In the next chapter, God's voice will come to Jonah again, telling him again to go to Nineveh. Jonah was spared a more serious punishment than three days' confinement in a fish, but he was not spared the task that God had set for him.

Did Jonah "get what he deserved"? In his treatment of Jonah, God may be turning this question around. What Jonah deserved may be ultimately less important than what God deserves, and what God deserves is obedience. God gave Jonah a second chance to obey.

Perhaps this is not a story about deserving at all but about God's love. God's love is for everyone, even disobedient people. If we are honest, we will admit that we are all disobedient people at times. If God only loved the obedient, there would be no human for God to love.

Maybe being in the belly of a fish would never have stimulated Jonah to repent, no matter how long he was in there. If so, God would have known that. In any case, God did not make Jonah wait in the fish until he was sorry about what he had done.

This does not mean that changing our ways is not important. Being sorry about what we have done and wanting to do better next time make a difference in our ability to understand and accept God's love and free us to respond to God's call to us with joy.

Furthermore, God having mercy on Jonah without Jonah having repented does not say anything about our chances for everlasting life with God if we do not repent. However, it does offer a hopeful word about God's relationship with us now, in this life. Even when other human beings might give up on us, God never gives up. God continues to love us and gives us second chances, even when no one else thinks we deserve it.

When is it appropriate to have mercy on someone else before they are sorry?

Delivering God, you help us out in times of trouble, even when our troubles are of our own making. Why do you love us so much, even when we run away from you or pretend that you are not there? Your love is so great; it is difficult for us to understand. Thank you for giving us second chances so that we may turn and serve you, as you have created us to do; in Jesus' name. Amen.

Daily Bible Study

God's Love for Nineveh

Purpose

To affirm that God's love extends even to our enemies

Hearing the Word

The Scripture for this lesson is printed below. The background texts are Jonah 3 and Nahum 1–3.

Jonah 3

¹The Lord's word came to Jonah a second time: ²"Get up and go to Nineveh, that great city, and declare against it the proclamation that I am commanding you." ³And Jonah got up and went to Nineveh, according to the Lord's word. (Now Nineveh was indeed an enormous city, a three days' walk across.)

⁴Jonah started into the city, walking one day, and he cried out, "Just forty days more and Nineveh will be overthrown!" ⁵And the people of Nineveh believed God. They proclaimed a fast and put on mourning clothes, from the greatest of them to the least significant.

⁶When word of it reached the king of Nineveh, he got up from his throne, stripped himself of his robe, covered himself with mourning clothes, and sat in ashes. ⁷Then he announced, "In Nineveh,

by decree of the king and his officials: Neither human nor animal, cattle nor flock, will taste anything! No grazing and no drinking water! [8]Let humans and animals alike put on mourning clothes, and let them call upon God forcefully! And let all persons stop their evil behavior and the violence that's under their control!" [9]He thought, Who knows? God may see this and turn from his wrath, so that we might not perish.

[10]God saw what they were doing—that they had ceased their evil behavior. So God stopped planning to destroy them, and he didn't do it.

Key Verse: God saw what they were doing—that they had ceased their evil behavior. So God stopped planning to destroy them, and he didn't do it. (Jonah 3:10)

Seeing the Need

I was in the third grade, showing off my geography knowledge to my babysitter. Holding a globe, I pointed out Washington, DC, near where we lived. I pointed out a few states, Canada, and Mexico. I showed her England, Egypt, and Israel. Then I pointed proudly to the broad expanse of the Soviet Union: "And that's where the people we hate live!"

She corrected me: "God loves those people, too, you know, and they didn't choose to be born there, just like you didn't choose to be born here. Just like you didn't choose to be born to a family who knows all about God's love. Some of the people who live there hate us but not all of them, and we don't need to hate them, either, if we remember that God loves them."

I was confused. How could God love Americans and also love Soviets? How could God love the people who had nuclear weapons pointed at me and my family? It was difficult to understand.

If God's love extends to our enemies, does that lessen God's love for us? Can we still trust God to take care of us and the people we love?

God's love is big enough for all of creation. God can love our enemies without that love for us diminishing in any way.

Living the Faith

Jonah's Enemy

It is no wonder that Jonah had run away from prophesying to Nineveh. He would have much preferred for Nineveh to have been destroyed with no warning. Nineveh was the capital of Assyria, and Assyria had repeatedly attacked Jonah's home country of Israel. Ultimately, the

Assyrians would destroy the nation of Israel utterly, forcing the Israelite people to abandon their homes and live away from the land God had given to them. Furthermore, they did not worship God. Jonah loved his country, and he did not want God to coddle his nation's enemies.

When we think of our enemies, our first thought might be enemies of our nation, nations or other groups of people who have threatened or attacked our own nation. As a child growing up near Washington, DC, in the 1970's and 1980's, when I heard Scriptures that talked about enemies, I first thought of the Soviet Union. This was a common reaction for Christians living in the United States during the Cold War. Many of us have the most difficulty accepting that God loves those who have declared war against our nation or against whom our nation has declared war.

Others of us might have the most difficulty accepting God's love for groups or individuals among us we feel have, by their words or actions, put our nation or our community in danger. We might characterize these persons' actions as reckless or selfish. We might have difficulty understanding how God could love people who seem only to love themselves, even to the point of endangering their own people. People do not need to be "outsiders" in order to be seen as our enemy.

Sometimes, the enemies that we least want God to love are personal enemies, people who have hurt us or who have hurt our friends or family members. They did not set themselves against whole groups of people, but they did plenty of damage on a smaller scale. They might have been strangers, or they might have been people we thought we knew well. Either way, it can be hard to accept that God could love someone who hurt us at close range.

If God loves us, isn't God angry with those people who hurt us? What would it take for God to be angry enough to stop loving them? Surely, there is a limit to the damage a person can do before God stops loving them.

The Book of Jonah was written after the people had returned from Exile. That means that its earliest readers were people who knew the worst of what Nineveh stood for: ruthless torture and slaughter of entire cities; displacement of entire nations of people. These large-scale disasters were made up of tens of thousands of individual heartbreaks.

Yet, this book was telling those first readers that God had loved the people of Nineveh, their worst enemies. The Assyrians were the worst enemies of the Jews since the Egyptians, but God did not want to destroy even the Assyrians without giving them a chance to repent. So God spoke to Jonah "a second time: 'Get up and go to Nineveh, that great city, and declare against it the proclamation that I am commanding you'" (Jonah 3:1-2).

If your pastor were preaching on God's love and forgiveness this morning, is there a way he or she could fill in this blank that you would find offensive? "God loves even _____ and desires for [him/her/them] to be saved."

Nineveh's Enemy

One morning, I was giving a talk to a group of United Methodist Women about the idea of being a family in Christ, sisters and brothers to one another. When I made the point that the people in our congregations were, like family, not necessarily the people we would have chosen, one of the women interrupted, "And they didn't choose you, either!"

This was not, I learned as we talked about it further, something that she meant for me to take personally. Instead, she meant in a general way that when we are considering our feelings about other people, we should also remember that other people have feelings about us, too.

Every group of people we call "they" and "them" call themselves "we" and "us." When we point an accusing finger and begin saying, "You . . . !" the person we are pointing at might raise his or her hands defensively and ask, "Who, me?" In the same way, those we consider outsiders have feelings about us and call us "them."

Looking at this story from Nineveh's perspective, we might wonder how God could love Jonah if God also loved Nineveh. Jonah had set himself so against that entire city that he had resisted taking God's word to them, lest they be given an opportunity to repent.

The Ninevites did not know how much Jonah hated them. Some of them might even have been grateful to Jonah for bringing this prophecy to them. If they had known, they might have wondered how it was possible for God to love Jonah so much while also loving them enough to warn them and to spare them.

When God loved Jonah, God was also loving the enemy of Nineveh. Because however much God loved Nineveh, God did love Jonah, too. God gave Jonah a chance to be a divine messenger. God kept trying to get through to Jonah, to help him understand God's love for all people, even his enemies. Jonah set himself against Nineveh, a city filled with people God loved, and God still loved him, too.

We find it difficult to understand how God could love certain people. At the same time, there are people who might find it hard to understand how God could love us.

Are there people God loves against whom we have set ourselves? Are there people whom we have threatened, harmed, or wished harm upon?

Is it harder to imagine that we may have done this as individuals, as communities, or as a nation? Are there people who might find it hard to understand why God would love us? Why or why not?

It is difficult to see ourselves as an enemy to someone else perhaps because we distance ourselves from our enemies, and we are not at all distant from ourselves. In order to imagine how a person could see us as their enemy, we have to imagine how we might look from the outside, at a distance.

However much anyone else might not understand it, God loves us. However much anyone else might wish that God would hate us, God loves us. Just as God's love extends to our enemies, God's love extends to us.

Is it possible not to be seen as an enemy by anyone, whether as an individual or by virtue of our membership in a group?

God's Enemies

In a sense, we are all at enmity with God. Another way to look at God's love for our enemies is that God loves God's own enemies.

Jonah and Nineveh were enemies to one another, but Jonah and the people of Nineveh had much in common, simply as human beings. The people of Nineveh loved their country and their families just as the Israelite people loved their own country and families. They had the same physical and emotional needs as the Israelite people. Most importantly, however, Jonah and the people he preached to were God's creation, God's creatures who were in rebellion against God. Jonah and the people of Nineveh were enemies to God.

Nineveh had set itself against God. Assyria, of which Nineveh was the capital, made regular raids on Israel, one of the two nations (together with Judah) populated by God's chosen people. The Assyrians did not honor or acknowledge Israel's God but worshiped Ishtar, a goddess who was ruthless in war, and they likewise were ruthless. Ishtar's temple was one of the major features of the city of Nineveh.

When Nahum was writing against Nineveh (in the century following when Jonah's story takes place), he pointed out that there would be no one to grieve Nineveh because that city had made so many enemies. Everyone would clap and cheer when Nineveh was finally destroyed (Nahum 3:7, 19). The Assyrians had killed and displaced so many people, destroyed so many cities and nations in the service of a bloodthirsty goddess; surely, they had set themselves against God.

Jonah had likewise set himself against God, disobeying the God he claimed to worship and serve. We have spent the previous two lessons examining Jonah's behavior. He ran away from his responsibility to God and showed absolutely no remorse.

When Jonah finally did obey, it is not clear that it was because of any change of heart. Instead, Jonah 4 records him as still feeling justified in his original motives for disobeying God. It seems most likely that Jonah finally went to Nineveh simply out of resignation because God would just keep hounding Jonah until he did what God had asked. This is not the behavior of one of God's friends. This is the behavior of an enemy.

When Paul reminds us that we have all sinned (Romans 3:9-23), that means we have all done things (and likely continue to do things) that are contrary to what God wants us to do. Every person sets himself or herself against God sometimes—at times unknowingly and at other times knowingly. Everyone is God's enemy in this sense, but Paul also writes that God does not turn away from us because of our sins but instead desires to be reconciled to us (2 Corinthians 5:18-20).

God understands that many of us are conflicted. Although we cannot seem to always do what God desires for us, nevertheless we continue to desire to please God, or at least we do sometimes. (Paul writes about this, too, for instance, in Romans 7:21-25.)

Some of us spend a great deal of time trying to understand what God desires for us. All of us studying this lesson devote at least some of our time to trying to understand or please God, or else we would not be bothering with Sunday school at all. There are people we would never suspect of caring about God at all who spend at least some of their time thinking about what God wants.

Extraordinarily, many of us (perhaps all of us?) continue to do things without even meaning to, sometimes even serving God while we are trying to resist God. Jonah, for instance, took the knowledge of God to the sailors on the boat as well as taking God's word to Nineveh. The Assyrians served God's purpose of punishing Israel, even though that was not their intent.

God sees into our hearts and sees that each of us is God's enemy at times. However, God also sees that each of is, or may be, God's friend. God loves each of us in our entirety, understanding where and how we are broken, while finding ways for us to become our better selves, to become the people God created us to be.

As a result of Jonah's message, "the people of Nineveh believed God" (Jonah 3:5). The king declared that all persons must " 'stop their evil behavior and the violence that's under their control.' He thought, Who knows? God may see this and turn from his wrath, so that we might not perish. God saw what they were doing—that they had ceased their evil behavior. So God stopped planning to destroy them, and he didn't do it" (verses 8-10).

What sorts of thoughts, words, or behaviors make a person God's enemy? What makes a person God's friend?

Merciful God, you have extended your hand in love even to our enemies. This can be so hard for us to accept that instead of turning in love to those who have hurt us, we turn on you in our anger. How could you love our enemies, Lord, and claim to be our friend? Help us to understand your love for those we cannot yet love, and help us to accept that your love for them is no more or less remarkable than your love for us; in Jesus' name. Amen.

Daily Bible Study

God's Pervasive Love

Purpose

To repent of our hard-hearted impulse to limit God's love and mercy

Hearing the Word

Jonah 4

[1]But Jonah thought this was utterly wrong, and he became angry. [2]He prayed to the LORD, "Come on, LORD! Wasn't this precisely my point when I was back in my own land? This is why I fled to Tarshish earlier! I know that you are a merciful and compassionate God, very patient, full of faithful love, and willing not to destroy. [3]At this point, LORD, you may as well take my life from me, because it would be better for me to die than to live."

[4]The LORD responded, "Is your anger a good thing?" [5]But Jonah went out from the city and sat down east of the city. There he made himself a hut and sat under it, in the shade, to see what would happen to the city.

[6]Then the LORD God provided a shrub, and it grew up over Jonah, providing shade for his head and saving him from his misery. Jonah was very happy about the shrub. [7]But God provided a worm the

next day at dawn, and it attacked the shrub so that it died. ⁸Then as the sun rose God provided a dry east wind, and the sun beat down on Jonah's head so that he became faint. He begged that he might die, saying, "It's better for me to die than to live."

⁹God said to Jonah, "Is your anger about the shrub a good thing?"

Jonah said, "Yes, my anger is good—even to the point of death!"

¹⁰But the LORD said, "You 'pitied' the shrub, for which you didn't work and which you didn't raise; it grew in a night and perished in a night. ¹¹Yet for my part, can't I pity Nineveh, that great city, in which there are more than one hundred twenty thousand people who can't tell their right hand from their left, and also many animals?"

Key Verse: Yet for my part, can't I pity Nineveh, that great city, in which there are more than one hundred twenty thousand people who can't tell their right hand from their left, and also many animals? (Jonah 4:11)

Seeing the Need

Is there anyone who frightens you? who angers you? whom you cannot forgive? who makes your skin crawl?

How would you feel if that person (or someone from that group of people) walked into your church for worship? Would it distract you from the sermon? Would you be able to sing the hymns? What if they came toward you to shake your hand during the passing of the peace? What if you were the greeter that day? What if you were helping the pastor serve Communion and that person came forward to receive?

Is there anyone you do not want anywhere near you? Is there anyone God does not want to be near?

God knows and understands our feelings, but our feelings and God's feelings are not always the same. God loves people whom we have trouble loving or cannot imagine ever loving, which can be difficult for us to understand and accept.

Living the Faith

Sun and Shade

What makes you angry? The answer to this question is not the same for everyone, of course. We all have different histories and different things that we care about. Some of us become angry about many different things, while others of us do not become angry easily or often. How angry we become may even depend more on who is causing the offense than on the offense itself.

In Jonah 4, Jonah becomes angry two times: when God decides not to destroy Nineveh (verse 1) and when God destroys the plant that was shading Jonah from the sun (verses 7-9). Do these two events have something in common? What could God taking action against the plant have to do with God refusing to take action against Nineveh?

Jonah was in a high, unprotected place, exposed to the sun and to hot desert winds. He tried to build a shelter for himself, but it must not have provided much cover. When a shady plant grew up in a single day beside the place where he had set up camp, Jonah did not question it; he was simply happy about it (verse 6). He took for granted this good thing that God had done for him.

It was not that Jonah deserved a comfortable place out of the hot sun. After all, Jonah had chosen this uncomfortable place for himself. Furthermore, he had chosen it peevishly, even disobediently. In spite of God's clear word that Nineveh would not be destroyed, Jonah had chosen this uncomfortable place because it would provide a good view if God did in fact destroy the city. In denial about what God wanted, Jonah put himself in an uncomfortable place.

Jonah did not wonder why God would reward his hard-headedness, but he did angrily protest when God decided not to go on rewarding him (shielding him from the hot sun). Perhaps Jonah had a point about Nineveh. Perhaps the people of Nineveh did not deserve to be shielded from the consequences of their sins, sackcloth and ashes notwithstanding (3:6-9). It is interesting, however, that Jonah did not worry about "not deserving" when it came to himself but only when it came to people he did not like.

Children growing up in the same family often behave in the same way. They are apt to protest angrily when a sibling gets "too much" attention or "too little" punishment, but they do not draw anyone's attention to any "unfair" treatment in their own favor. This may be intentional, but it may as likely be that the child simply does not notice unfairness unless it seems not to be in their favor.

Are we the same way? Do we only notice it when other people receive benefits they do not deserve? Do we fail to notice when we receive privileges or opportunities that we did not somehow earn?

God's love and mercy can make us uncomfortable: God's capacity for love and forgiveness is so much greater than our own. We cannot even love ourselves as thoroughly as God loves us, and for some people, a limited idea of divine love begins with denying that love to themselves. It takes a leap of faith to simply accept that God's love is abundantly available to others without diminishing that love for us. God's love goes beyond what we can understand or justify. It may even seem unreasonable to us.

Is there anything about God's love that you find difficult to understand or accept?

Right and Left

When I was not quite five years old, my mother tried to teach me to tell left from right. Her lessons were complicated by my three-year-old sister, who was fascinated by a more familiar pair of opposites: "right" and "wrong." My mother would point to a foot and ask me if it was my right or my left. If I answered, "Right," my little sister would gleefully call out, "Wrong!" Today as an adult, I still hesitate when asked by a doctor to lift my right leg or when instructed by my GPS to turn to the left. I still expect that my first instinct will be the wrong one.

Jonah 3:10 gives us one reason for God having chosen not to destroy Nineveh: God saw that the people had repented. "God saw what they were doing—that they had ceased their evil behavior. So God stopped planning to destroy them, and he didn't do it." However, this repentance must have been short-lived.

The early readers of this book would have known that this same capital city went on, after the time of Jonah, to wage merciless war on many places, including Israel. It was after their supposed change of heart and behavior that the Assyrians laid waste to Israel and scattered that nation's population. Perhaps it is because of this that we are given an additional reason in 4:11.

When I read that "one hundred twenty thousand people . . . can't tell their right hand from their left," my first thought is of children. While some adults like me struggle with distinguishing right from left, telling the difference is a skill most six-year-olds have mastered. If young children are the people meant by this expression, then perhaps in verse 11 God is saying something like, "I understand that you are angry at the people of Nineveh, Jonah, but what about the children and the animals? Would you have me destroy these innocents, just because of the actions of a representative collection of adults?"

This is a question we have continued to ask in our own time. In times of war, is it appropriate to target entire cities (including necessarily many innocent noncombatants) in order to stop our enemies from destroying even more lives? Like some modern military strategists, Jonah might well have weighed the loss of innocent Ninevites and still preferred for the entire city to be destroyed.

Assyria was incredibly destructive to many different peoples, and might, in Jonah's mind, better have been stopped. Furthermore, Nineveh's children were going to grow up to become part of the Assyrian war machine themselves, he likely reasoned. Why would God choose not to stop them in Jonah's day instead of allowing this nation to go on wreaking havoc for another century?

Was God weighing the lives of innocent children and animals in the decision not to destroy "a few bad apples"? Is this the question that God is posing to Jonah (and to us) at the end of the book? Or, when we read God's question in this way, are we reading our contemporary questions and concerns into a Scripture verse that is asking something different than what our modern ears expect to hear?

What if "people who cannot tell their right hand from their left" did not mean children at all? What if this phrase was meant to refer to all of the inhabitants of Nineveh?

Taken this way, the phrase presents a different concept of innocence. Arguably, in this case, God would not have been describing innocence at all. Instead, this phrase (as applied to an entire culture) simply describes incapacity: The Assyrians were incapable of discerning the correct path to take in life. Or, as my sister might have simplified the translation as a three-year-old: When saying "right from left," God may be meaning "right from wrong."

In our own culture, "ignorance of the law is no excuse." We have special legal categories for people who we believe cannot be expected to know the difference between right and wrong: children, people with certain mental illnesses, or those whose IQs fall below a certain level. Everyone else should know what constitutes acceptable behavior.

When a person commits a certain crime, it is perhaps obvious that they are incapable of choosing the right path to take. Someone who is able to make good choices would not choose to kill another person, defraud them, or otherwise injure them; but because they ought to be able to make good choices, we hold them accountable. If we never correct anyone unless they are capable of having made a better choice, then it is possible that we would never punish anyone at all. People would just go on hurting other people without anyone or anything to stop them.

If "one hundred twenty thousand people who can't tell their right hand from their left" means all of the people of Nineveh, including the king of Assyria and all of his counselors, then God is arguing against punishing them because they did not know any better. It is easier for us if the expression means children because then we do not have to struggle with what it might mean for God to give the Assyrians a reprieve based solely on their inability to make moral decisions, on them being as self-interested and incapable of good decision-making as cattle.

We might not be as eager as Jonah to see such a city utterly destroyed, but shouldn't it get its comeuppance or at least be prevented from doing any more damage to its neighbors? When I remember that God's "thoughts are not [my] thoughts, / nor are [God's] ways my ways" (Isaiah 55:8, NRSV), I wonder which is the way in which God intends us to understand Jonah 4:11?

Why did God spare Nineveh?

Anger and Pity

We begin to hear about Jonah's anger in Jonah 4:1. God questions Jonah's anger twice, in verses 4 and 9. In the CEB translation printed above, God asks, "Is your anger a good thing?" The NRSV similarly translates this as "Is it right for you to be angry?"

Many times we read the implicit answer to this question as no, but God does not answer the question and neither does the book's author. The question was asked of Jonah, and he refused to answer the first time. Is it possible for God to do right not to be angry and for Jonah to do right to be angry? Perhaps what God protested was not so much that Jonah was angry as that Jonah believed God ought to have still been angry. Jonah was demanding that God should feel angry, too.

When God asked about Jonah's anger a second time, Jonah answered, "Yes, my anger is good—even to the point of death!" (verse 9). This did not make much sense. Good to the point of death?

Some Bible scholars believe that it would be more accurate to translate these questions and answers in a more neutral way, not inquiring about the rightness of Jonah's feelings but instead probing the intensity of his feelings. The Jewish Publication Society's translation of the Hebrew Bible renders Jonah 4:9 this way: "Then God said to Jonah, 'Are you so deeply grieved about the plant?' 'Yes,' he replied, 'so deeply that I want to die.' "

Either way, God never told Jonah that his feelings of anger were wrong, but we may feel that Jonah's feelings were over the top. Could a single withered plant seriously be enough to make him so angry he could die? Maybe that is the point for us, the readers. We do not share Jonah's feelings! We do not even totally understand those feelings. In the same way, we cannot assume that everyone understands our own feelings, much less shares them. We cannot even assume that God, who understands all things, necessarily shares our feelings. God cares about our feelings, but that does not mean God always feels just the same way as we do.

Chapter 4 began with Jonah's anger, but God shifted the conversation to pity. When Jonah looked at Nineveh, all he could feel was anger. However, when God looked at Nineveh, God felt pity. This was a hard lesson for Jonah: In the end, God's feelings were not the same as Jonah's feelings.

How God feels about someone else is not for us to choose. God will decide how to act in the world.

In the story recorded in the Book of Jonah, Jonah resisted God's love for the Ninevites, and he was afraid of what God would do because of that love. Jonah did not trust God to be God. This caused Jonah all kinds of trouble.

After giving so much space for Jonah's protests, it is fitting that God is given the last word in the Book of Jonah; but it is interesting that this last word is in the form of a question. God's words call for a response.

What will be our answer? Will we let God decide whom to care for and how to care for them; or will we, like Jonah, futilely insist on trying to stand in God's way?

How has your understanding of God's love changed over time?

Lord, we love you, and we trust you; but sometimes, when your ideas are different from our own, we become confused and upset. Changing our hearts and changing our minds is uncomfortable for us. Forgive us for demanding that you limit your love in the same ways as our own love is limited. Forgive us for trying to make you in our image instead of allowing you to shape us into your own image. Give us the courage to love as you love; in Jesus' name. Amen.

Daily Bible Study

God's Urgent Call

This summer, lessons in ADULT BIBLE STUDIES follow the theme, "God's Urgent Call." This theme reminds us that God continues to speak to us through the written Word. God calls ordinary people from diverse backgrounds to make a difference. From the days of the judges to the prophets to the early church leaders, God called, and the faithful answered. The student book writer is Barbara Derrick. The writer for the teacher book is Gary Thompson.

Called to Be Strong
The first four lessons this quarter introduce the era of the judges. The Book of Judges continues the history of Israel after Joshua's death. God raised up a series of national leaders called judges. Empowered by God, judges delivered the people from their enemies.

Calling of Prophets
The five lessons in this quarter's second unit look at how God called various prophets at different times for specific purposes. Included in this unit are the calls and responses of Moses, Isaiah, Jeremiah, Ezekiel, and Amos.

Calls in the New Testament
The final four lessons this quarter demonstrate that God continued to work through ordinary people. Their witness reminded the early church that God assures the success of those who will answer God's call. The unit highlights the calls of Stephen, Peter, Philip, Ananias, and Paul.

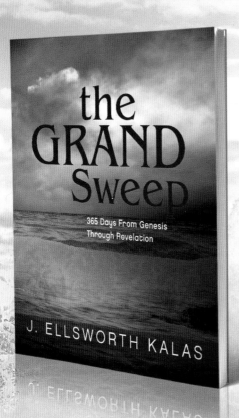

Study the whole Bible in a year with J. Ellsworth Kalas

Every day:

Read Scripture.

Respond. Pray.

Published by

Growing in Life, Serving in Faith

The Grand Sweep guides readers through the Bible in a year by having them read three to four chapters daily. The Psalms and Proverbs are scattered throughout the readings as devotional elements. Because the reading plan moves through the Bible in biblical sequence, readers grasp the grand sweep of the Scriptures—something missed in most Bible studies. Daily readings are manageable, allowing someone just beginning a serious devotional life to have the positive experience of developing new spiritual discipline. Individuals can start reading at any time of the year. When the year of reading ends, they will have a grasp of the biblical story from beginning to end and a stronger devotional life.

Kalas also provides a faithful daily summary of readings, but with a devotional quality to encourage warmth of spirit as well as knowledge of mind. Included is a reflection from son David Kalas and selected quotations from Kalas' 35 books.

Cokesbury